**AMERICAN
SIGN
LANGUAGE
DICTIONARY
FOR
BEGINNERS**

AMERICAN SIGN LANGUAGE DICTIONARY FOR BEGINNERS

A VISUAL GUIDE WITH 800+ ASL SIGNS

TARA ADAMS

PHOTOGRAPHY BY **JAMES BUETI**

ROCKRIDGE
PRESS

For general information on our other products and services or to obtain technical support, please contact our Customer Care Department within the United States at (866) 744-2665, or outside the United States at (510) 253-0500.

Rockridge Press publishes its books in a variety of electronic and print formats. Some content that appears in print may not be available in electronic books, and vice versa.

TRADEMARKS: Rockridge Press and the Rockridge Press logo are trademarks or registered trademarks of Callisto Media Inc. and/or its affiliates, in the United States and other countries, and may not be used without written permission. All other trademarks are the property of their respective owners. Rockridge Press is not associated with any product or vendor mentioned in this book.

Interior and Cover Designer: Carlos Esparza
Art Producer: Megan Baggott
Editor: Anna Pulley
Production Editor: Jax Berman
Production Manager: Riley Hoffman
ASL Model: Jocelynn Only

Photography © 2020 James Bueti.
Styling by Bethany Eskandani.

Hardcover ISBN: 978-1-68539-702-9
    Paperback ISBN: 978-1-68539-713-5
    eBook ISBN: 978-1-63878-701-3
R0

CONTENTS

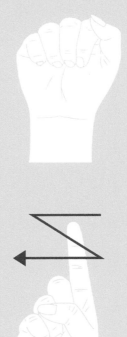

INTRODUCTION

Welcome. I am so glad you have decided to journey into the richly expressive language of American Sign Language (ASL). If you are a beginning signer, you have selected a fantastic resource. The vocabulary word selections and language basics overview have been compiled specifically for you to use in the earlier stages of your ASL development.

As a Deaf person and a mother of two hard-of-hearing children, I have a personal interest in more people in the community learning to sign. The more people there are in the community who know sign language, the more access my children, fellow community members, and I have to the world around us. It allows us to have more meaningful relationships and connections with our hearing counterparts. It allows us more opportunities to be seen (heard) and valued by others. Perhaps someday, humanity will develop a way to communicate without barriers such as hearing loss or speaking different languages. Until then, thank you for choosing to learn the language that grants Deaf, hard-of-hearing, and verbally challenged people the greatest access.

I have been teaching community ASL classes for over 18 years. Those who sign up for my courses are learning for a variety of reasons. Here are some of them:

- I have a family member, friend, coworker, partner, employee, client, teammate, or neighbor who is Deaf or hard of hearing.

- I (or a family member) am losing my hearing and want to learn signs that will help decrease frustration and raised voices.

- I have or work with a child who is nonverbal or who has special needs that make verbal communication difficult.

- I love the idea of learning a visual language and want to communicate with my hands/body.

Regardless of your reason for learning ASL, or where you are learning it, I hope that this book will be a helpful vocabulary resource guide to accompany you through the initial stages of your signing journey.

Part One

BASICS OF SIGNING

American Sign Language (ASL) is a structured method of communicating, just like any other language. The critical difference is that it's not expressed verbally, nor is it received through auditory means. ASL is expressed through designated signs and gestures for words and concepts, as well as through rule-based hand/body movements and facial expressions. ASL has its own unique lexicon, as well as its own syntax and grammar rules. As you study ASL, it is important to remember that English and ASL are two very distinct languages. Although this book is written in English and the words are listed alphabetically, it's helpful to avoid direct comparisons between the two. The more you are able to release your reliance upon English to learn and make sense of ASL, the easier it will be to fully internalize and master the language.

When you use an English dictionary, you don't expect it to teach you how to communicate in English. You use it as a reference guide for specific vocabulary words, pronunciations, and usages. This dictionary has a similar aim. Although we will go over some basic ASL building blocks and a brief introduction to the community behind the language, the information provided is not intended to be a comprehensive guide or a stand-alone resource.

The following section is meant to give you a crash-course overview, to be expanded upon through additional, more in-depth language resources.

1

A BRIEF HISTORY OF AMERICAN SIGN LANGUAGE

Gestures and signs have been used to communicate since the beginning of humankind, long before spoken languages developed. Although spoken language has become the predominant method of communicating, advanced sign language systems have evolved in countries and cultures throughout the world to give Deaf and hard-of-hearing people the opportunity to participate and exchange thoughts in a language that is fully accessible to them.

ASL is the language used by the Deaf community in the United States, Canada, and several other foreign countries that have adopted and modified it to fit the needs of their own people and cultures. Like other languages, ASL developed organically to meet the needs of those who use it. It was heavily influenced by early home-based signs, as well as French Sign Language, which was brought to America by a Deaf French educator named Laurent Clerc. Clerc was recruited to America by Thomas Hopkins Gallaudet, who wanted a way to formally educate American Deaf children. Together they founded the first school for the Deaf in Connecticut in 1817.

Recognition of ASL as an official language, rather than just a gesture/pantomime communication system, finally began in the 1960s, thanks in large part to the intense research and literary publications of William Stokoe, an American linguist and long-time professor at Gallaudet University. ASL is now widely accepted and offered as an official foreign language at thousands of high schools and universities throughout North-America.

As you dive into ASL and the people who use it, the term "Deaf community" will pop up frequently. Many people ask, "Do you have to be Deaf to be part of the Deaf community?" Absolutely not! This community can include family members, friends, ASL interpreters, Deaf educators, and deeply dedicated students of ASL. Members of the Deaf community share a sense of camaraderie and understanding not only through a shared language but also through commonly shared life experiences. Deaf schools, clubs, athletic teams, and community events (both online and in person) are cherished avenues for bringing the Deaf community together, and they have, over time, given rise to a robust American Deaf culture.

Deaf culture is enriched through the shared life experiences of Deaf and hard-of-hearing individuals, as well as those who are committed to being part of their lives. Deaf culture thrives and enriches lives through artistic expressions, poetry, storytelling, traditions, norms, and, most importantly, ASL. ASL has given people with hearing loss the opportunity to access and connect with others in the world around them. One of the first questions a Deaf person may ask another signer when they first meet is "Are you Deaf or hearing?" If the answer is "Deaf," there is an immediate understanding and connection based on an embodied understanding of navigating life in a sound-based world without the ability to fully hear. These relationships are critical for Deaf and hard-of-hearing people, as they give them a sense of belonging and validation. It is difficult for others who have never experienced life without full access to sound to fully understand this unique journey.

You may have noticed that the word Deaf has been capitalized throughout this book. Those who identify as Deaf, with a big D, are those who embrace ASL and Deaf culture and are involved in their local Deaf communities. It is an identity label rather than a medical one. A person who identifies as Deaf might be considered "hard of hearing" by their medical provider, based on their diagnosed level of hearing loss, yet if their hearing loss is embraced with pride, they are immersed in the Deaf community, and are fluent in ASL, they typically self-label as "big D" Deaf. This should always be a personally selected label. There are many more millions of Deaf or hard-of-hearing people throughout the country who have a hearing loss but do not know or use ASL and are not immersed in the Deaf community. That is okay! Everyone has the right to their own sense of identity in the way that brings them the most fulfillment and validation.

THE WIDE WORLD OF ASL

Sign language can also be very helpful for individuals who are not Deaf or hard of hearing. These include people with special needs who are pre- or nonverbal, or those who encounter communication barriers that make spoken language difficult. Typically, signers in this category use signs as an additional tool in conjunction with spoken English. Therefore, they are not actually using the full language of ASL; rather, they are using signs already developed for ASL to facilitate improved communication experiences. Using signs to enhance spoken English has been shown to be highly beneficial for individuals in this unique group, since they are not fully dependent on visual communication due to lack of hearing. However, because ASL and English have different grammatical rules and syntax, true ASL cannot be expressed in fullness when used simultaneously with spoken English. It is important to understand that when signs are used along with spoken English, much critical linguistic content is inadvertently and unavoidably left out. When this happens, individuals who do not have full access to spoken language due to hearing loss are unable to fully access deep and meaningful communication.

DIALECTS

As you study ASL, keep in mind that there are a wide variety of accents and signing styles, just as in spoken language. Watching a variety of videos of native ASL signers and getting involved with your local signing community will greatly nourish your receptive skills and help you recognize and learn subtle nuances and signing styles. Live community interactions in your area will introduce you to location-specific sign variations, as well as some dialects, including Black American Sign Language (BASL). If you are studying ASL in a foreign country that has adopted ASL and modified it to fit their unique location and culture, it is especially important that you get involved in your local signing community.

FURTHER STUDY

Since this book is just a supplemental reference for learning ASL, I highly encourage new signers to also study and learn the rich culture and history of the community it serves through other sources as well. Find out how name signs are assigned, how Deaf people make phone calls, how Deaf parents "hear" their babies cry at night, why Deaf people tend to congregate in well-lit areas such as kitchens, how modern technology has changed the lives of Deaf and hard-of-hearing people, and how you can be most supportive and inclusive of those who have hearing loss. You will discover a whole community that has adapted and evolved to function and thrive in a noisy world without a dependence on sound. If you are wondering how to get more involved with the Deaf community and meet other signers, make sure to check out the Resources section (page 319) for further guidance. For true mastery of the language, including comprehension of even the most subtle nuances, it is important to study ASL in-depth from a variety of sources, including live interactions with local signers.

ABOUT THE LANGUAGE

Because ASL is expressed with the body rather than vocally, it utilizes tools and techniques that are different from spoken languages. Something as simple as raising your eyebrows or tilting your head can turn a statement into a question, or indicate a new topic is being introduced.

In the next section, I'll introduce some of the main building blocks of ASL, including some of the basic grammatical rules. We will then cover classifiers, fingerspelling, and numbers basics, as well as a few other key word groupings such as days, months, and colors, before we move on to the dictionary itself.

BUILDING BLOCKS OF SIGNING

The following terms and structures will help you interpret and understand the signing instructions in this book.

SENTENCE STRUCTURE AND TENSES

One of the most important things to understand about ASL is that it mainly utilizes a topic-comment sentence structure. Although different from English, this type of sentence structure is actually similar to many other major spoken languages. When you express a thought in ASL, unless it is a question, you typically start by signing the topic or main point, followed by the related details. In English you might say, "I am going to the store." In ASL, if "store" is the topic of your expression, then you would sign STORE I GO WILL. Notice the tense, WILL, comes at the end of the ASL sentence. The placement of tenses, indicated in ASL through the signs WILL (future), NOW (present), and FINISHED (past), is another grammatical difference between ASL and English.

FIVE PARAMETERS OF SIGNS

There are five distinct parameters that go into each sign. Some signs will be different in all five parameters, while some signs will be nearly identical except for one parameter.

Handshape

Each sign incorporates specific hand-shapes. Sometimes you may have signs that are done in the same location with the same movement, but the handshape is different and therefore represents a different word. Here is an example:

RED

CUTE

Location

Each sign is made at a specific location on the body or within your surrounding signing space. The signs for MOM and DAD are the exact same handshape, movement, and palm orientation, but are initiated at different reference points on the body for male (dad) or female (mom).

MOM

DAD

Movement

Each sign has a particular movement. The signs for FUN and FUNNY have the same handshape, location, and palm orientation, but they have different movements that indicate whether you are saying FUN or FUNNY.

Orientation

Orientation refers to the direction that your palm is facing when you make a sign. For some signs, your palm may face away from you, and for other signs, your palm may face toward you, downward, or to the side. Two examples are YOURS and MINE:

FUN

YOURS

FUNNY

MINE

Nonmanual Markers (NMMs)

Nonmanual markers are a very important part of ASL, and believe it or not, they are necessary tools for conveying grammar, emotion, and other linguistic information. Some signs may be exactly the same in all ways except a shake of the head to show negation (no), or a nod to show affirmation (yes), such as the signs for UNDERSTAND and DON'T-UNDERSTAND. With these signs, the only difference is the head shaking or nodding to show that you do understand or you do not understand.

UNDERSTAND

DON'T-UNDERSTAND

FACIAL EXPRESSION

Facial expression is used to convey other linguistic information as well. When you are introducing a new topic, you typically raise your eyebrows, which signals to the person you are communicating with that a new topic is being initiated.

You also use facial expressions to indicate the asking of questions. A yes/no question (Y/N?) is accompanied by raised eyebrows and a forward head tilt. WH questions (WH?) such as who, what, when, where, why, which, and how are accompanied by furrowed eyebrows and a slight sideways head tilt known as a WH expression.

Facial expression is very helpful in showing emotional intensity. There is a difference between the emotions behind the words MAD and FURIOUS. By using a more intense expression of anger and also a more strongly emphasized movement, you can convey the more intense emotion of fury.

HAND DOMINANCY

The alphabet, numbers, and many signs in ASL are done with one hand, or utilize one hand to perform a movement while the second hand plays a support role. Typically your dominant hand—the one that you write with—is going to be your main signing hand. For sign clarity and economy of motion, it is important that you avoid switching back and forth between hands for dominancy.

The nondominant hand, when used in signs where it performs just a support role, tends to take a neutral handshape. The most common handshapes you will see in these signs are B, A, S, C, O, 1, and 5.

VERB DIRECTIONALITY AND NOUN/VERB PAIRS

There are a few different ways in which verbs can be modified in ASL. One way is through sign directionality. For example, consider the sign for HELP. If I modify the sign with a forward motion, I am now saying CAN I HELP YOU? If I sign HELP in the direction of myself, I can communicate WILL YOU HELP ME? Notice which image shows a WH? expression and which one does not.

CAN I HELP YOU?

WILL YOU HELP ME?

HELP

There are also many signs for nouns that can be modified to make them function as verbs. For example, the signs for AIRPLANE and FLY as well as CAR and DRIVE. In these cases, the noun is signed with a double movement, then the associated verb is signed with a single forward movement.

AIRPLANE

FLY

CAR

DRIVE

INDEXING (TALKING ABOUT PEOPLE WHO ARE NOT PRESENT)

In ASL, indexing (pointing) is used to refer to nouns that are present in the surrounding environment of the signers. This is one of the many ways ASL utilizes signing space, which is the area within a signer's comfortable reach, to convey context.

So, what about when we are discussing nouns, such as people, who are not present? If I want to tell you something about my mom, but she is not within our current eye view, I will first sign MOM, then I will point downward toward a specific location, perhaps to my right or left, to establish a reference point for MOM. Pointing downward clarifies that I am not pointing to someone who is actually present. Once I have a reference point for MOM, I can use pronouns and possessives in the direction of this reference point to indicate SHE, HER, HERS. I can even put additional people on my storyboard and indicate interactions between them through plural pronouns and possessive indexes like THEY, THEM, and THEIRS. Once the topic changes and new people are discussed, the former "storyboard" is wiped clean, so to speak, and a new one begins.

Another difference to note between ASL and English is that ASL pronouns are not gender specific. The same sign is utilized for YOURS, HERS, and HIS.

CHRONOLOGICAL ORDER OF EVENTS

In ASL, events are typically discussed in chronological order. In English, they are often expressed in reverse. For example: In English you might say: "I am going to the gym after work." In ASL, you would list the events in the order that they occur by signing WORK FINISHED, GYM I GO.

CLASSIFIERS

Classifiers are used in many languages to accompany and expand on nouns, especially when a noun is being counted. Due to the visual nature of ASL, the importance of classifiers cannot be overstated. This will become clear to you as you go deeper into your studies. Without classifiers, ASL as a language would be incomplete.

Classifiers are handshapes and/or rule-based pantomime. The purpose of classifiers is to give additional information about nouns and verbs, such as movement, location, shape, manner, and size. There are different types of classifiers, such as descriptive, semantic, elemental, body/body parts, instrumental, locative, and quantitative. Classifier predicates in ASL are used abundantly, especially in descriptions,

directions, and storytelling. Deep study of ASL classifiers through more comprehensive sources is strongly encouraged. Here are some of the most common classifier handshapes in ASL, as well as some basic examples of how to use them:

CL is an abbreviation for classifier. Following the letters CL you will see a colon, then a letter or number which indicates the handshape for that particular classification.

CL:1

Use for: person walking, referencing

CL:2

Use for: legs, eyes, two people walking side by side

CL:2 (modified)

Use for: small animals or bugs scurrying, people sitting

CL:3

Use for: vehicles, three people walking side by side

CL:4

Use for: hair descriptions, liquid running, flowing or trickling, lines of people, stripes, fencing

CL:5

Use for: bodies of water, movements or congestions of nouns

CL:5 (modified)

Use for: piles, scoops, claws, rashes, placement of structures, crowds

CL:A

Use for: knocking, heart thumping

CL:B

Use for: flat surfaces such as windows, doors, floors, aisles, shelves, walls, paths, roads

CL:C/O

Use for: poles, pipes, columns, canisters, buckets, binoculars, telescopes, tunnels

CL:C (modified)

Use for: medals, large buttons, badges, dishes, tattoos, small bodies of water

CL:F

Use for: buttons, coins, jewelry, piercings, eyeballs, spots, dots, round flat objects

CL:G

Use for: stacks of paper, layers, short hair, to show thickness (nouns)

CL:I

Use for: string, wire, noodles, cords, lines (not lines of people)

CL:H

Use for: straps, labels, bows, belts, tags, tongues, animal ears, Band-Aids, tape, paintbrushes

CL:L

Use for: pictures, rugs, placemats, 90-degree angles, rectangular objects such as receipts, checks

CL:S

Use for: banging, heads, hooves

CL:X

Use for: spraying, hunched over people, scratches, hooks

CL:X (modified)

Use for: keys, zippers, popsicles/suckers, turning dials

FINGERSPELLING

In ASL, the alphabet is presented with your dominant hand using specific handshapes for each letter. Fingerspelling is used mainly for names, titles, abbreviations, places, and words that do not have a specific sign. Fingerspelling is also used for measurements and abbreviations such as: IN (inch), OZ (ounce), LB (pound), ST (street), PL (place), and RX (prescription). Many states and cities use their abbreviations for their identifying name sign. To learn the signs for places in your geographical area, ask members of your local Deaf community.

For some words, the fingerspelled version of the word, often modified for economy of motion, becomes the dominant way to sign the word. These are called loan signs or lexicalized signs. Some other commonly fingerspelled words in ASL are: BACK, BUS, TRUCK, VAN, UBER, TAXI, CLUB, JOB, ALL, FIX, ICE, STYLE, OK, RENT, BAND, BID, BURN, SORE, FLU, NAP, RUG, ZOO, TOYS, SALE, DEBIT, SO, WILD, CHIPS, DVD, RISK, LOTTERY, WOW, BUT, and RX.

Fingerspelling is also used to sign the months of the year. For January (JAN), February (FEB), August (AUG), September (SEPT), October (OCT), November (NOV), and December (DEC), you sign the abbreviations. MARCH, APRIL, MAY, JUNE, and JULY are spelled out completely.

As you will see in the photos, fingerspelling is done mainly with your palm facing outward, in front of your body (but not touching your body), in the space in front of the shoulder of your dominant hand. The exceptions to this are G and H, which are done with the palm facing inward, and P and Q, which are done with the palm facing down.

Avoid bouncing your hand with each letter and keep your hand in place as you string the handshapes together to form words. If you are fingerspelling more than one word at a time, a slight pause will indicate separate words. For example, if you were fingerspelling New York, you would sign NEW (slight pause) then YORK. Make sure to always use your dominant hand and avoid switching back and forth between hands. If there are double letters in a word, the most common way to sign them is by making the handshape for the letter and sliding it slightly to the side (away from your body).

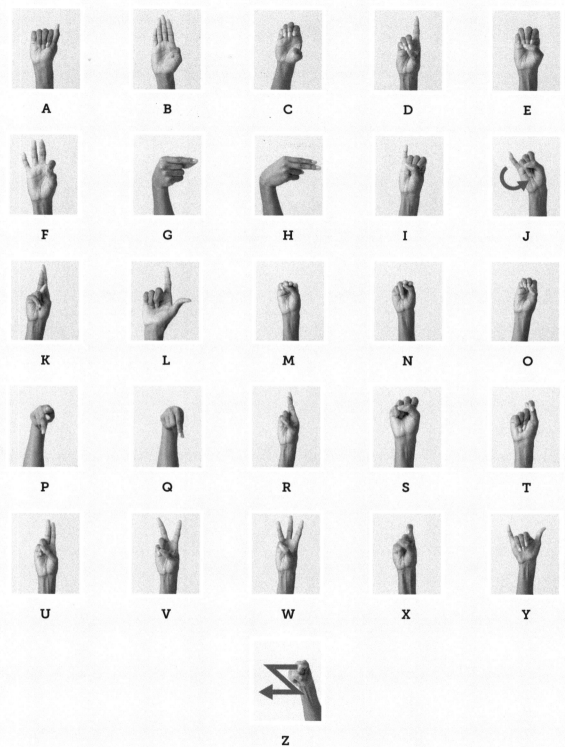

NUMBERS

Numbers in ASL are all done on one hand. Numbers 1 through 5, if presented by themselves, are done with the palm facing inward. If they are used in a number combination, then they are performed with the palm forward, like most of the other number signs. Numbers 11 through 15 are always signed with your palm facing your body.

Once you learn the signs for numbers 1 through 30 and the signs for HUNDRED, THOUSAND, and MILLION, then the rest of the numbers are basically just combinations of these signs. Check with more in-depth sources to learn other subtle nuances and variations when it comes to signing numbers.

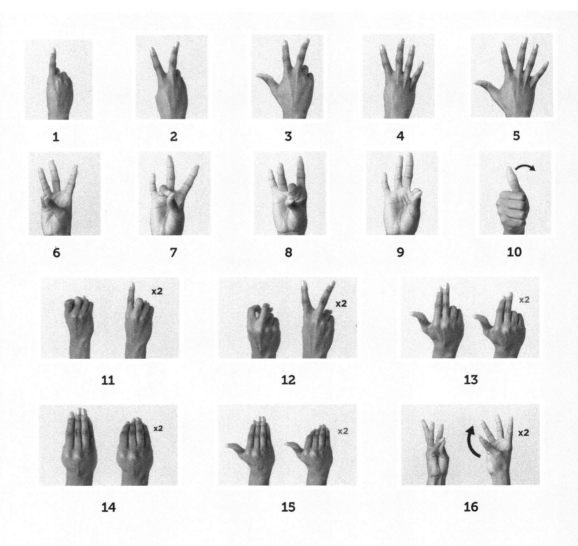

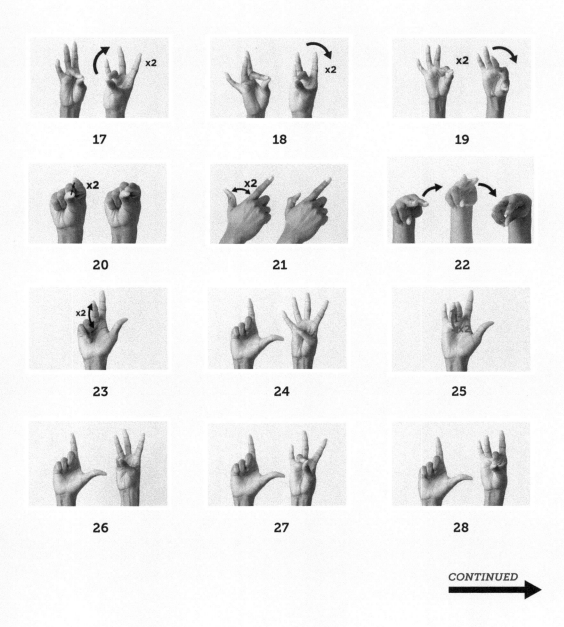

17

18

19

20

21

22

23

24

25

26

27

28

CONTINUED →

29

30

40

50

60

70

80

90

100

THOUSAND

x2

MILLION

NUMERICAL INCORPORATION

Sometimes numbers, up to 9, can be incorporated into specific signs. This is typically referred to as numerical incorporation. For example, if I wanted to sign 8 WEEKS, I would simply modify the base sign for WEEK using the number 8 handshape. You will see a lot of numerical incorporation in time-related signs.

Once you pass number 9, the movement of the subsequent numbers makes it difficult to incorporate the number into the sign. People often refer to this rule in ASL as the Rule of 9.

THE BODY TIMELINE TO CONVEY PAST AND FUTURE TIME REFERENCES

Think of your body as being the center of a timeline. Time signs that are modified to move forward, in front of your body, indicate that they are in the future. Time signs that incorporate a movement toward the back of your body indicate that they are referencing the past. For example, take that sign for 8 WEEKS. If I add a backward or forward movement to this sign, I am referencing 8 WEEKS AGO or IN 8 WEEKS.

8 WEEKS

DAYS OF THE WEEK

MONDAY: Make an M handshape with your dominant hand, palm facing inward, and move it in a small, circular, clockwise motion.

TUESDAY: Make a T handshape with your dominant hand, palm facing inward, and move it in a small, circular, counterclockwise motion two times.

WEDNESDAY: Make a W handshape with your dominant hand, palm facing inward, and move it in a small, circular, counterclockwise motion.

THURSDAY: Fingerspell the letters T-H with your dominant hand. Make a small, circular, clockwise motion with the H.

FRIDAY: Make an F handshape with your dominant hand, palm facing inward, and move it in a small, circular, counterclockwise motion.

SATURDAY: Make an S handshape with your dominant hand, palm facing inward, and move it in a small, circular, counter-clockwise motion.

TIP: Each sign, Monday through Saturday, begins with the first letter of that day of the week.

SUNDAY: With both hands in flat open handshapes, palms facing outward at eye level, make small circles with both hands in opposite directions.

COLORS

The colors RED, PINK, and ORANGE are signed on the chin. BLUE, GREEN, PURPLE, and YELLOW are signed using the first letter of the color and are done with a repeated, outward twisting motion from the wrist.

To show color vibrancy or shade, the sign for the color may be done faster and with stronger intensity to show darker or bolder hues, while pastel colors are usually done with slower and more delicate movements.

RED

PINK

ORANGE

Squeeze fist two times.

YELLOW

BLUE

BLACK

GREEN

BROWN/TAN

PURPLE

WHITE

Starting with your dominant hand in a flat handshape against your chest, pull the hand away from your chest, and change the handshape to an O.

GREY

Move hands back and forth, passing through the spread fingers two times.

HOW TO USE THIS BOOK

When you look up a sign in this dictionary, you'll see a still image that represents it. Most signs, however, are not stationary and require movement. We tried to capture the critical apex of each sign, then added arrows or lines to represent directionality and movement, as well as repetition of movements. Some signs require contact with more than one part of the body or include more than one handshape; in these cases the sign may be presented with two images to show both contact points.

You will also find text descriptions of each sign, which are best understood if read while referencing the image. In almost every description we will say what handshape the sign uses. Most hand-shapes are described using a letter or number, such as C, K, or 1. Other common handshapes are: flat open hand, flat O and claw, index finger, and fist. We'll also mention what direction the palm(s) are facing: palms facing inward (toward the body), palms facing outward (away from the body), palms facing down, palms facing each other, etc. Oftentimes in a sign, the palm orientation will change with a movement. A large percentage of signs are done in the space in front of your middle to upper torso.

Some signs represent more than one English word. When this happens, you will find, in most cases, the English word that comes first alphabetically is where the sign will be displayed in the dictionary. For example, the sign for BILL represents the English words *owe*, *debt*, *bill*, and *due*. You will find the image under the word BILL, because B comes first alphabetically. The words OWE, DEBT, and DUE, when looked up alphabetically, will appear with a note: "See: Bill/Debt/Due/Owe."

Some words/concepts have more than one possible sign, which we may mention in the Tip sections. If you get involved with your local Deaf community, you will spot some of these sign variations. These variations are normal, but you should always defer to your local Deaf community when you come across signs that are different from the ones we show in this book.

As you are looking at the sign illustrations in this book, keep in mind that all signs are made from the signer's perspective. The model in this book is right handed, so if you are right handed, you will be producing the signs in reverse. If you are left handed, then you make the signs as if you are looking at yourself in the mirror.

Part Two

A–Z

@

Make an A handshape with your dominant hand, palm facing outward, and move it in a circular, clockwise motion.

TIP: This sign looks a lot like the symbol it represents.

ABANDON (See: Leave [abandon], page 178)

(See: Leave [abandon], page 178)

ABLE/POSSIBLE

With both hands in fists or A handshapes, palms facing down, bounce your hands up and down two times from the wrists.

ACCEPT

With both hands in open-ended O handshapes, palms facing inward and fingers pointed to the side, position them just inside the shoulder blades. Close the hands simultaneously into flat O handshapes.

TIP: This sign looks like something being absorbed or accepted into your body, the way a sponge absorbs water.

ACCIDENT/MISTAKE

Make a Y handshape with your dominant hand, palm facing inward, and move it from one side of the chin to the other in one smooth movement. This can also be used to say WHOOPS.

ACCOMPLISH

Raise your nondominant hand and make a 1 hand-shape, palm facing outward. With your dominant hand, start with a claw handshape, palm facing outward, and move it toward the other hand, ending in a fist as soon as you reach it.

ACCURATE (See: Right [correct/accurate], page 233)

ACCUSE/BLAME/FAULT

Make a flat handshape with your nondominant hand, palm facing down. Make an A handshape with your dominant hand, the thumb pointing upward. Drag the bottom of your dominant fist forward, across and past the top of your nondominant hand.

TIP: This is a directional sign, and you can move your dominant hand in the direction of who is being accused.

ACQUIRE (See: Get/Receive/Acquire, page 140)

ACROSS (See: After/Across, page 28)

ADD/ADDITION

Make a flat O handshape with your nondominant hand, palm facing inward, as if you are holding a card in front of you. With your dominant hand, start with an open handshape, palm facing inward, positioned below your nondominant hand. Move it upward to touch your nondominant hand while closing your fingers into another flat O handshape.

TIP: Think of holding up a note card then adding another one below it.

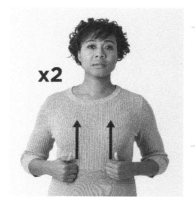

ADDRESS

With both hands in A handshapes, palms facing inward, touch your chest just inside your shoulders with two quick upward movements.

ADJUST (See: Change/Modify/Adjust/Alter, page 73)

ADOPT

Make 5 handshapes with both hands, palms facing down, then close both hands into fists as you raise them upward.

TIP: It kind of looks like you are picking something up—perhaps a baby carrier.

ADVICE/COUNSEL

Make a fist or flat handshape with your nondominant hand, palm facing down. With your dominant hand in a flat O handshape or loosely closed fist, touch the thumb to the top of your nondominant hand and slide the hand forward over the wrist two times, opening the fingers with each sliding movement.

AFRAID/SCARED

With both hands in 5 handshapes in front of your chest, palms facing inward and fingertips pointing at each other, move your hands quickly toward each other and back again one or more times.

AFRICA

Make a flat O handshape in front of your body with your dominant hand, palm facing outward. You will trace the shape of Africa by opening your hand into a wide C and closing your hand back into a flat O handshape as you reach the tip of the continent. This entire sign is done in a smooth, fluid motion.

AFTER/ACROSS

With both hands in flat open handshapes, position your nondominant hand with the palm facing down. Move your dominant hand, palm facing to the side, over the top of your nondominant wrist.

TIP: Think of crossing over a bridge.

AFTERNOON

With both hands in flat handshapes, position your nondominant arm in front of the body horizontally. Rest the elbow of your dominant arm on the fingertips of the nondominant hand, with the dominant arm at a 45-degree angle.

TIP: Think of the sun midway through the sky.

AGAIN/REPEAT

With both hands in flat open handshapes, position your nondominant hand with the palm facing up. With your dominant hand, palm facing inward, make an arching movement, then land your fingertips in the middle of your nondominant palm.

AGE/OLD/HOW-OLD

With your dominant hand, start with a claw handshape or fist in front of your chin, and lower the hand as your handshape changes to an S.

AGE has two quick downward movements, OLD has one long downward movement, and HOW-OLD is signed by making a WH? expression (page 7) while signing AGE.

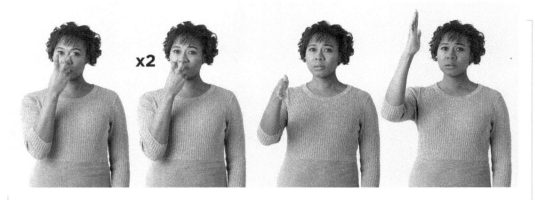

AGNOSTIC

This sign is a combination of DOUBT (page 105) and GOD (page 144). Your dominant hand first signs DOUBT with the hand in a V handshape at eye level, palm facing inward. Bend the fingers two times. Then sign GOD with your dominant hand in a flat B handshape, palm facing to the side. Start with your hand positioned horizontally near your head on your dominant side. Bring the fingertips up, ending with your hand positioned vertically.

AIRPLANE/FLY

Make an open handshape with your dominant hand, palm facing outward, and fold down your middle and ring fingers, keeping the other three fingers open. Slide the hand forward in two quick movements.

To sign the verb, FLY, make the same handshape with your dominant hand, but instead of two quick forward movements, make one long forward movement.

ALARM/SCHOOL-BELL

Make a flat handshape in front of your body with your nondominant hand, palm facing outward or to the side. Make a 1 handshape with your dominant hand and knock the fist against your nondominant palm two times.

TIP: Think of the clanging of a clapper inside of a bell.

ALIVE (See: Live/Alive, page 182)

(See: Live/Alive, page 182)

ALL/WHOLE

With both hands in flat handshapes, hold your nondominant hand in front of your body, palm facing inward. With your dominant hand, circle all the way around the other hand, then spoon the palms with both facing inward.

TIP: This sign looks like you are scraping the edges of a large bowl with your hand like a spatula. This word is also commonly fingerspelled.

ALL-DAY

Hold your nondominant arm in front of your body, palm facing down and touching the elbow of your other arm. With your dominant hand, start with your fingers pointing straight up, then fold your arm down until it lands directly on top of your nondominant arm, both palms facing down.

TIP: Think of the movement of the sun as it travels across the sky.

ALL-DONE (See: Finished/All-Done, page 128)

ALL-NIGHT

Make a flat open handshape with your nondominant hand, palm facing down. Hold this arm in front of your body with your fingertips touching the inner elbow of the other arm. With the fingers of your dominant hand pointing down, bring your arm and flat open palm upward until they touch the bottom of your nondominant arm.

TIP: Think of the movement of the sun as it travels around the opposite side of the earth during the night.

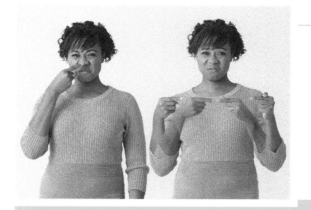

ALLERGY/ALLERGIES

This sign has two parts. First, touch your nose with the index finger of your dominant hand. Second, touch both of your index fingers together, then move them away from each other quickly.

TIP: The movement of this sign is like two magnets pushing away from each other.

ALLOW/LET

With both hands in flat handshapes in front of the body, palms facing each other, move both hands forward and slightly upward.

TIP: Think of marking a path to allow something to pass through.

ALMOST/EASY

With both hands in flat open handshapes, palms facing up, brush the fingertips of your dominant hand along the back of your nondominant fingertips one time.

If you repeat this movement two times, it becomes the sign for EASY.

ALONE

Make a 1 handshape with your dominant hand, palm facing inward, and move it in a small side-to-side rocking motion two times.

TIP: Think of your index finger as someone swinging all by themselves.

ALTER (See: Change/Modify/Adjust/Alter, page 73)

ALWAYS

Make a 1 handshape with your dominant hand, palm facing inward, and move your arm in a circular, lasso-like motion from the elbow joint, making two rotations.

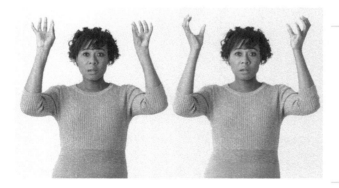

AMBULANCE

With both hands in bent 5 handshapes, palms facing outward and hands above the head, twist your wrists back and forth.

AMERICA/UNITED-STATES

With both hands in 5 handshapes, the fingers straight and interlaced and the palms facing inward, move your interlaced hands in a counterclockwise circle.

TIP: United States is fingerspelled (U-S). You can combine US and AMERICA to say UNITED STATES OF AMERICA.

AMERICAN-SIGN-LANGUAGE/ASL (NOUN)

Fingerspell the letters A-S-L, but do this in one smooth motion, with the L coming out in a flicking motion.

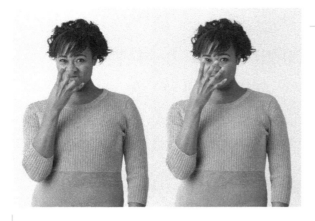

ANGRY/GRUMPY/MAD

Make a 5 handshape with your dominant hand in front of your face, palm facing inward, then stiffen and bend your fingers into a 5 claw handshape.

GRUMPY is done by flexing the fingers a couple of times while making this sign.

TIP: Intensity of facial expression and sign movement is what expresses different degrees of the emotion of anger.

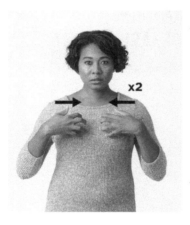

ANIMAL

With both hands in flat bent handshapes, palms facing inward, touch the fingertips of both hands just inside your shoulder blades and move the backs of your palms toward each other, repeating two times, similar to a bird flapping its wings.

ANNIVERSARY/CELEBRATE

Hold both hands at shoulder height, palms facing each other, and pinch the thumb and index fingers together. Make circular motions with both hands.

TIP: A celebratory expression goes well with this sign.

TIP: You can communicate specific types of celebrations by identifying the occasion before signing CELEBRATE.

ANNOY/BOTHER/INTERRUPT

With both hands in flat open handshapes, palms facing inward, knock the bottom side of your dominant hand into the space between the finger and thumb of your nondominant hand two times.

If you make just one knocking movement, this becomes the sign for INTERRUPT.

ANY/ANYONE/ANYWHERE

Make an A handshape with your dominant hand, palm facing up, and turn your hand until the palm is facing down.

For ANYWHERE, add the sign for WHERE (page 305) by making a 1 handshape with your dominant hand, palm facing outward. Shake your finger side to side. For ANYONE, add a 1 (page 14).

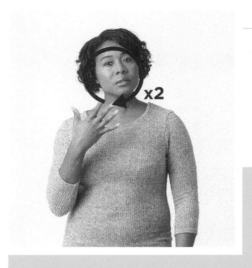

APPEARANCE/ATTRACTIVE

Make a 5 handshape with your dominant hand and position it at eye level, palm facing inward. Move your hand in a repeated circular motion.

TIP: To communicate GOOD LOOKING or ATTRACTIVE, sign GOOD (page 145) before APPEARANCE. To sign GOOD, with both hands in open handshapes, palms facing up, place the tips of the fingers of your dominant hand on your chin. Bring the hand down to land on the palm of the nondominant hand.

APPLE

Make an X handshape with your dominant hand and touch the back of your finger knuckle to your cheek, twisting your hand forward two times.

APPLY/APPLY-TO/ APPLICATION/ APPLICABLE/TO-FILE

Make a 1 handshape with your non-dominant hand held in front of the body, palm facing to the side. Make a V handshape with your dominant hand, palm facing to the side. Begin the sign with your dominant hand positioned vertically, and then bring it down so that the V fingers go around the 1 finger, palm facing down.

APPOINTMENT/ RESERVATION

With both hands in A hand-shapes, hold your nondominant hand out in front of your body at a 45-degree angle, palm facing down. Hold your dominant hand just above your nondominant hand and circle around it in a clockwise direction to form a half circle in the air. Then drop your dominant hand down on top of your nondominant wrist.

APPROXIMATELY

Make a 5 handshape with your dominant hand, palm facing outward, then move it in a circular, counterclockwise motion two times.

TIP: This sign can also be used to communicate that you are making a rough estimate when you do not have an exact quantity.

AREA/FIELD/GROUND

Make a 5 handshape with your dominant hand, palm facing down, and move it in a circular, counterclockwise motion two times.

This sign can also be used for GROUND, as in playground, FIELD, or other bodies of ground space.

ARGUE

Point the index fingers of both hands at each other, then move your hands up and down two times from the wrists.

ARRIVE

Make flat open handshapes with both hands, palms facing up. Hold out both hands, with your dominant hand starting above your nondominant hand, then move your dominant hand forward and downward till it lands on the nondominant palm.

TIP: Think of your dominant hand arriving at or landing on your nondominant hand.

ART

Make a flat handshape with your nondominant hand and hold it in front of your body, palm facing up. With your dominant hand in an I handshape, make a squiggly line down the center of your nondominant hand.

TIP: Think of drawing on a piece of paper with your pinky finger.

ASIA

Make an A handshape with your dominant hand, palm facing down or outward. Move it downward and out to the side in a circular motion, but as your hand starts the upward motion of the circle, make a 5 handshape and end above where your A hand started.

ASK (REQUEST, FORMAL)

With both hands in flat handshapes, bring your palms together and pull them closer to the body.

TIP: Think of making the gesture many people use for prayer.

ASK (QUESTION)

Make an X handshape with your dominant hand, and wiggle your index finger up and down one time for ASK and two or more times for QUESTION(S).

TIP: This is a directional sign. If your palm is facing toward the person you are talking to and you move the sign in their direction, then you can show that you are asking them a question(s). If you turn your palm to face your body and move the hand toward you, then you are showing that you are the one being asked a question(s). You can also add a Y/N? expression (page 7) to say DO YOU HAVE A QUESTION(S) FOR ME?

ASL (See: American-Sign-Language/ASL [noun], page 35)

AT-LAST (See: Finally/At-Last, page 126)

ATHLETE (See: Compete/Competitor/Athlete/Race, page 82)

ATTEMPT (See: Try/Attempt, page 289)

ATTEND/GO

With both hands in 1 handshapes, palms facing outward and index fingers pointing up, make quick forward and back movements with both hands two times. Your index fingers will point downward with each forward movement.

By making just one forward movement, you are signing GO.

ATTRACTIVE (See: Appearance/Attractive, page 38)

AUNT

Make an A handshape with your dominant hand, palm facing outward. Hold it near the side of your cheek next to your chin, but not touching your face, and make two small circling or twisting motions.

AUSTRALIA

With both hands in 8 hand-shapes, palms facing down, bring your hands up and forward in an upward arch, ending the arch by opening your hands into 5 handshapes.

AVERAGE (See: Medium/Average, page 190)

AWESOME

Hold your nondominant hand in a 1 hand-shape with the finger pointing forward. With your dominant hand, start in a 5 hand-shape and close into an S handshape as you slide the hand across the top of the nondominant index finger.

AWFUL/TERRIBLE

Make an 8 handshape in front of your body with your dominant hand, palm facing to the side and fingers pointing upward, then flick your middle finger from the tip of your thumb.

TIP: You can also do this sign with both hands for emphasis.

BABY

Hold both arms in front of your body as if cradling an infant. Make a side-to-side rocking motion.

BACK-AND-FORTH

Make an open A handshape with your dominant hand, palm facing to the side and the thumb pointing upward, then move your hand in, out, and then back in.

BAD

Make a flat handshape with your dominant hand, palm facing inward, and touch your fingertips to your lips/chin. Then quickly reverse the palm forward, moving your hand down and away from the body.

BAKE

Hold out your nondominant hand, palm facing down. Make an open handshape with your dominant hand, palm facing up, and slide it underneath your nondominant hand.

TIP: The motion looks like sliding a tray of cookies into the oven.

BAND-AID

Make a fist with your nondominant hand, palm facing down. With your dominant hand in an H handshape, pull the fingertips across the back of your nondominant hand.

TIP: This sign looks like your fingers are tracing a Band-Aid on the back of your wrist.

BANKRUPT (See: Broke/Bankrupt, page 65)

BARELY

Make an F handshape with your dominant hand, touch the side of your forehead with your pinched fingers, and move your hand forward.

TIP: This sign looks as if you are plucking a tiny hair off your head.

BASEBALL

Hold your hands together in closed fists, one above the other, as if you are holding a baseball bat, and make a couple of small swinging motions.

BASKETBALL

With both hands in 3 handshapes, palms facing each other, rock your hands back and forth.

TIP: There are several other signs for BAS-KETBALL. Always defer to your local Deaf community.

BATH

With both hands in A handshapes, palms touching inside your shoulder blades, move your hands up and down simultaneously over your chest.

TIP: This sign looks as if you are scrubbing yourself.

BATHROOM/RESTROOM/TOILET

Make a T handshape with your dominant hand, palm facing outward. Shake your hand side to side.

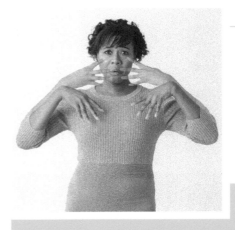

BAWL/SOB

With both hands held horizontally in 4 handshapes, palms facing inward and the tips of your index fingers under your eyes, trace two or three lines down the face as if multiple tears are falling.

TIP: Make sure you have a very anguished look on your face.

BEACH

Hold up your nondominant hand in a flat hand-shape, palm facing down. Make a flat O handshape with your dominant hand and rest it on top of your nondominant hand. The fingers of your dominant hand should be pointing toward you. Make a 5 handshape with your dominant hand as you slide it closer to your body, then slide it back into the O handshape again. Repeat two times.

TIP: This sign looks like waves crashing upon a shore.

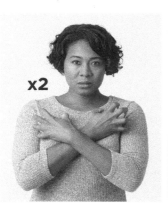

BEAR

With both hands in claw handshapes, cross your arms over each other and scratch your shoulders twice.

TIP: It looks like you are giving yourself a big bear hug.

BEARD

Make a C handshape with your dominant hand, palm facing inward, touch your fingertips to the back of your jaw, and slide them down to your chin.

TIP: This can also be done with both hands or modified to show different kinds of beards.

BEAUTIFUL

Make a 5 handshape at the side of your face with your dominant hand, palm facing inward, then move it to the other side of your face as you close your fingers into a flat O handshape.

TIP: To emphasize, make the movement bigger and more intense.

BECOME/BE

With both hands in flat open handshapes, palms pressed together—one facing outward and the other facing inward—twist and turn the wrists while maintaining contact so the palms are facing the opposite direction.

TIP: You can also use this sign for GET when used in expressions like I HOPE YOU DON'T GET SICK.

BED

Make a flat handshape with your dominant hand and touch your palm or back of your hand to the side of your cheek, as if lying down on a pillow.

TIP: This can also be done with both hands.

BEER

Make a B handshape with your dominant hand, palm facing outward, and hold it next to your dominant cheek. Make small up-and-down or circular motions with your hand.

BEFORE (PRIOR TO)

With both hands in flat handshapes, palms facing inward, put your dominant hand directly behind the other and move it toward you while the non-dominant hand stays in place.

BEFORE (PAST)

Make a flat handshape with your dominant hand positioned above your shoulder, palm facing inward, and make a backward gesture as if waving at someone behind you.

TIP: You can indicate that something is further in the past by making a larger backward gesture or increasing the repetitions of the movement.

BELIEVE

Make a 1 handshape with your dominant hand, touch your index finger to the side of your forehead, and then clasp both hands together in front of your body.

BEST

Make a flat handshape with your dominant hand, palm facing inward and positioned horizontally. Touch your fingertips to your chin, then move your hand upward as you make an A handshape.

BEST-FRIEND (See: Friend/Best-Friend, page 135)

BETTER

Make a flat handshape with your dominant hand, palm facing inward and positioned horizontally. Touch your fingertips to your chin, then move your hand out to the side as you make an A handshape.

TIP: This is very close to the sign for BEST (page 52), except that the A handshape does not lift up.

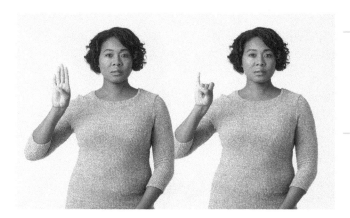

BI/BISEXUAL

Fingerspell the letters B-I with your dominant hand.

BICYCLE

Make fists with both hands and hold them in front of your body, palms facing down, as if holding the handlebars of a bicycle. Now rotate your fists in alternating circles, as if pedaling a bicycle.

BIG/LARGE

With both hands in bent L handshapes, palms facing each other, move the hands away from each other, out to the sides. Your mouth makes a "CHA" sound as you perform this sign.

TIP: Although this is the general sign, there are many other ways to sign BIG that are proportionate to the noun they describe. You always make the "CHA" sound with the mouth to indicate largeness.

BILL/DEBT/DUE/OWE

Make an open handshape with your nondominant hand, palm facing up. With the index finger of your dominant hand, touch the center of your nondominant palm in a firm repeated movement.

TIP: It looks as if you are gesturing to someone to put money in your hand.

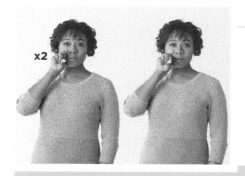

BIRD/CHICKEN

With your dominant hand, make a G hand-shape held against the side of the cheek with the fingers near the mouth. Pinch your index finger and thumb together two times.

TIP: Imagine your fingers are the beak of a bird chirping.

BIRTH

With both hands in flat handshapes, position your nondominant hand in front of your chest or belly, palm facing inward. Touch the palm of your dominant hand to your belly, then move your hand away from your belly until it lands in the palm of your nondominant hand.

TIP: Refer to your local Deaf community for other ways to sign BIRTH.

BIRTHDAY

Make a 5 handshape with your dominant hand, the middle finger extended forward and palm facing inward. Place the tip of the middle finger on your chin and then bring it down to touch your chest.

BLAME (See: Accuse/Blame/Fault, page 26)

BLANKET

With both hands in flat bent handshapes and positioned in front of your chest, palms facing down or inward, bring both hands up to touch close to your neck in a repeated movement.

TIP: There are other ways to sign this word. Defer to your local Deaf community.

BLIND

Make a bent V handshape with your dominant hand, palm facing inward, and tap the tip of the two bent fingers to your dominant cheek, just below your eye.

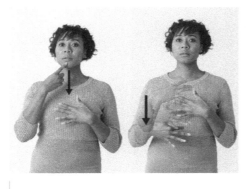

BLOOD

This sign has two parts. First, sign RED (page 19) by stroking the index finger of your dominant hand down your chin. Second, with both hands in 5 handshapes positioned horizontally, your dominant hand in front of your nondominant hand and palms facing inward, keep your nondominant hand still while wiggling the fingers of your dominant hand in a downward motion.

BOAT

With both hands in flat handshapes, palms facing up and positioned side by side so that your hands resemble a boat, bounce your hands up and down a couple of times.

TIP: Think of your hands as a boat crashing through waves.

BODY

With both hands in flat open handshapes, touch the palms to your chest. Move both hands down and touch them to the body again at a lower position.

BONE

With both hands in bent V handshapes, palms facing inward, cross your arms at the wrists and tap the wrists together two times.

BOOK

With both hands in flat handshapes, palms facing up, bring them together like two sides of a book and open them while keeping the pinky fingers together, as if they were the binding. Open and close your hands two times.

BORED

Touch the index finger of your dominant hand to the side of your nose and make a twisting motion. You can also make this sign bigger for emphasis.

BORROW/LOAN

With both hands in K handshapes, place one fist on top of the other and move them either toward the body or away from the body, depending on if you are the giver or the receiver.

TIP: This is a directional verb. If you are the receiver, move the hands toward your body; if you are the giver, move the hands toward whoever is the receiver.

BOSS

Make a claw handshape with your dominant hand and tap your dominant shoulder two times with your fingertips.

BOTH

Make an open fist with your nondominant hand, palm facing inward. Make a U or V handshape with your dominant hand and slide the fingers down through the open fist of your nondominant hand.

BOTHER (See: Annoy/Bother/Interrupt, page 37)

BOWL

With both hands in cupping handshapes, palms facing up, bring your hands together into a bowl shape, then move them upward and slightly apart.

BOY

With your dominant hand in front of your forehead, make a pinching movement with all of the fingers while moving your hand away from your forehead.

TIP: Think of pulling on the rim of a baseball cap.

BOYFRIEND

This sign is a combination of BOY and FRIEND (page 135). Your dominant hand first signs BOY in front of the forehead: Make a pinching movement with all the fingers and move the hand away from the forehead. For FRIEND, with both hands in X handshapes, the palm of your nondominant hand facing up and the palm of your dominant hand facing down, hook your index fingers together briefly and then flip your hands so that your dominant hand is now facing up and the nondominant hand is facing down, again hooking your index fingers together briefly.

BRAG

With both hands in A handshapes, palms facing down, touch your thumbs alternately to your hips.

TIP: A prideful expression goes well with this sign.

BRAIN

Make an X handshape with your dominant hand and tap the index fingertip to the side of your forehead two times.

TIP: It looks as if you are tapping at your brain inside your skull.

BRAINSTORM

Make a 1 handshape with your dominant hand and sign THINK (page 279), touching your index finger to the side of your head. Next, make both hands into fists up near your head, palms facing down, and open your hands into loose 5 handshapes, moving them forward alternately, as if you were taking ideas from your head and throwing them down onto paper.

BRAVE/CONFIDENT/HEALTHY

With both hands in 5 handshapes, touch both hands to your shoulders, and then pull away from your shoulders as your hands close into fists.

TIP: For BRAVE and CONFIDENT, the hands tend to move out to the sides; for HEALTHY, they tend to move forward in front of the body.

BREAD

Hold up your nondominant hand in a flat open handshape, palm facing inward. Make a bent B or bent flat handshape with your dominant hand and run the tips of the fingers down the back of your nondominant hand two times.

TIP: Think of tracing the slices in a loaf of bread.

BREAK (FRACTURE)

With both hands together in S handshapes in front of your body, palms facing down, twist your wrists in opposite directions as if you were snapping a stick in half.

BREAK (TIME-OFF)

Your nondominant hand is in the flat B handshape, with the palm facing to the side. Your dominant hand is in the flat B handshape, with the palm facing down. Slide the dominant hand between the middle and ring fingers of the non dominant hand.

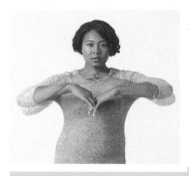

BREAK-DOWN (ENGINE)

With both hands in claw handshapes, palms facing each other, interlock your fingers and drop your hands downward as your fingers break away from each other.

TIP: Think of your hands as interlocked gears breaking apart.

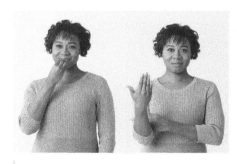

BREAKFAST

This sign is a combination of EAT (page 110) and MORNING (page 196). Sign EAT with your dominant hand in the flat O handshape. Touch your fingertips to your mouth once. Sign MORNING with both hands in the flat B handshape. Your nondominant arm is held horizontally in front of the body. Your dominant hand palm is facing up. Place the fingertips of the nondominant hand on top of the crook of the elbow of the dominant hand. Raise the dominant arm from horizontal to slightly up, just under a 45-degree angle.

BREAK-UP (See: Disconnect/Break-Up, page 100)

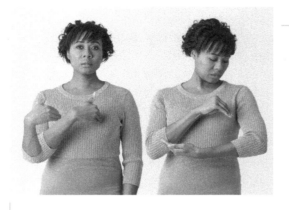

BREASTFEED

This sign is a combination of BREAST and EAT (page 110). Your dominant hand first signs BREAST with a flat bent handshape. Tap your fingertips to your chest just above each breast. Then quickly transition to signing EAT. Hold your nondominant arm out, as if cradling a baby, and with your dominant hand in a flat O handshape, sign EAT at the area where the baby's mouth would be if it were in your arms.

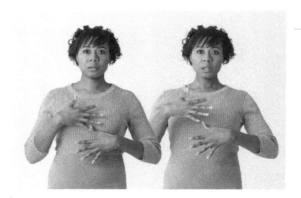

BREATH/BREATHE

With both hands in 5 handshapes, palms resting against the chest and stomach, move the hands away from the body a few inches and then bring them back to the chest and stomach.

TIP: Imagine the lungs expanding and contracting. You can also show that someone is short of breath by repeating the movement quickly several times while showing a panting expression.

BREEZE (See: Wind/Breeze, page 308)

BROKE/BANKRUPT

Make a flat bent handshape with your dominant hand, palm facing down, and make one chopping motion on the neck.

TIP: This sign is sometimes made with both hands for emphasis.

BROTHER

Make an L handshape with your nondominant hand, palm facing to the side or inward, and hold it in front of your body. Make an A (or L) handshape with your dominant hand, placing the thumb at the side of the forehead. Bring your dominant hand down on top of your nondominant hand, making an L handshape as it lands.

BRUSH-TEETH

Make a 1 handshape with your dominant hand in front of your mouth, palm facing down. Pull your lips back to expose your teeth and make brushing movements across your teeth as if your fingertip were the brush head.

BUDDHISM

Make a 7-8 handshape with your non-dominant hand, palm facing to the side. This means both your middle and ring fingers are touching your thumb, and your pinky and index fingers are extended. Make a 1 handshape with your dominant hand, palm facing inward, and tap the circled fingers of your non-dominant hand two times.

BUG

Make a 3 handshape with your dominant hand, palm facing to the side, then touch your thumb to your nose and bend your other two fingers two times.

BUSINESS

Make a B handshape with your dominant hand and a fist with your nondominant hand, palms facing down, and brush your dominant hand back and forth across the nondominant fist.

BUSY

With both hands in B handshapes, hold your non-dominant hand, palm facing down, in front of the body. Brush the wrist of your dominant hand, palm facing outward, back and forth across the side of your nondominant hand.

BUTTERFLY

With both hands in flat handshapes, palms facing inward, cross your hands over each other and link the thumbs. Then, make a flapping motion with the rest of the fingers.

TIP: In this position, your hands resemble an actual butterfly.

BUY/SHOP/SHOPPING

Hold out your nondominant hand in a flat hand-shape, palm facing up. Make a flat O handshape with your dominant hand, palm facing up. Place your dominant hand on the palm of your nondom-inant hand, sliding your dominant hand forward, as if taking money out of your hand and handing it to a cashier.

You can turn the sign for BUY into the sign for SHOP by repeating the movement.

CALENDAR

Hold up your nondominant hand in a flat hand-shape, palm facing inward. With your dominant hand, make a gesture that looks like you are lifting the page of a calendar and flipping it over the top and down the back of your nondominant hand.

CAMPING/TENT

Hold up just the pinky and index fingers of each hand and touch the fingertips to each other. Pull your hands downward and away from each other. Repeat the movement two times for CAMPING (verb) and once for TENT (noun).

TIP: The shape and movement of this sign looks similar to an actual tent.

CAN (VERB)/ABLE

With both hands held out in A handshapes or fists, palms facing outward, drop your wrists down in a sharp movement.

TIP: ABLE/POSSIBLE (page 24) is signed by repeating this movement two times.

CAN (NOUN) (See: Cup/Glass/Can, page 91)

CANDY/DIMPLES

Make a 1 handshape with your dominant hand, touch your index finger to your cheek, next to your mouth, and make a double twisting motion.

If you smile while making this sign, you can use it to sign DIMPLES.

CAN'T

With both hands in 1 handshapes, palms facing down, position one index finger just above the other, then move the upper finger down, knocking the lower finger as you pass by it.

TIP: Think of a child reaching up to touch a hot stove and a parent knocking their finger out of the way and saying, "You can't touch that!"

x2

CAR/DRIVE

Hold out both hands in fists, as if they were grasping a steering wheel, and move them alternately up and down as if you were swerving from side to side.

To sign the verb DRIVE, move the fists in a smooth forward motion rather than a swerving motion.

x2

CAREFUL/TAKE-CARE-OF

With both hands in K handshapes, stack one fist on top of the other and move them together in a forward circular motion two times.

CAT

Make an F handshape with your dominant hand, palm facing outward. Place the pinched fingers at the corner of your mouth and pull out to the side to suggest whiskers.

TIP: There are several other ways to sign CAT. Defer to your local Deaf community.

CENTER/CENTRAL

Hold out your nondominant hand in a flat hand-shape, palm facing up. Make a flat bent handshape with your dominant hand and position it just above your nondominant hand, making a partial circular motion before placing your fingertips in the center of your nondominant palm.

TIP: Think of marking the center of your palm.

CENTS

Make a 1 handshape with your dominant hand, palm facing inward, and touch your index finger to the side of your forehead, then move it a few inches away from the forehead without changing the palm orientation.

CERTIFICATE/CERTIFIED/LICENSE

With both hands in C handshapes, palms facing each other, tap the tips of the thumbs together two times. If you start with L handshapes instead, it becomes the sign for LICENSE.

If you make one tapping movement instead of two, it becomes the sign for CERTIFIED or LICENSED.

CHAIR/SIT

With both hands in U handshapes (the U handshape on the dominant hand is often bent), palms facing down, tap your dominant fingers on top of the nondominant fingers two times.

If you make the tapping movement once instead of twice, this sign represents the verb SIT.

CHALLENGE

With both hands in A handshapes, thumbs up and palms facing down or inward, knock the knuckles together one time.

CHANGE/MODIFY/ADJUST/ALTER

With both hands in X handshapes, palms facing each other, bring the wrists together and twist your hands while maintaining contact so that the position of your hands is reversed.

CHARGE/COST/FEE/FINE/PRICE/TAX

Hold out your nondominant hand in a 5 handshape, palm facing inward or to the side. Make an X handshape with your dominant hand and run your index knuckle down the palm of your nondominant hand.

TIP: This sign looks somewhat like holding the trigger of a barcode scanner.

CHASE (See: Follow/Chase, page 131)

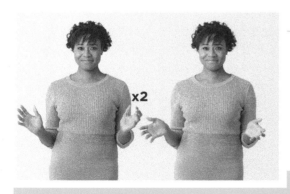

CHAT/TALK

With both hands in claw handshapes held out to the sides, palms angled up, shake both hands downward two times at an inward angle.

TIP: Think of how Deaf people chat with their hands rather than their mouths.

CHEAP

With both hands in flat handshapes, hold your nondominant hand horizontally, palm facing to the side. With the palm of your dominant hand facing down, swipe the side of the hand across your nondominant palm as it drops.

CHICKEN (See: Bird/Chicken, page 55)

CHILD/CHILDREN

To sign CHILD, use just one hand, lowering it down once as if resting your hand on the head of a small child.

For CHILDREN, make flat handshapes in front of the body with both hands, palms down. Make a downward tapping motion with both hands, then bounce your hands farther apart and tap downward again.

CHOCOLATE

Hold out your nondominant hand in a fist or flat handshape, palm facing down. Make a C handshape with your dominant hand, touch the back of the thumb to the back of your nondominant wrist, and move your dominant hand in a circular, stirring motion.

TIP: Imagine the circular motion of stirring melted chocolate.

CHOICE/CHOOSE

Hold out your nondominant hand in front of you, palm facing inward, in either a V or a 5 handshape. With your dominant hand, pinch your thumb and index fingers together and touch two fingers on your nondominant hand, then move the pinched fingers upward.

TIP: Imagine you are picking a finger.

CHORE (See: Responsible/Duty/Obligation/Chore, page 232)

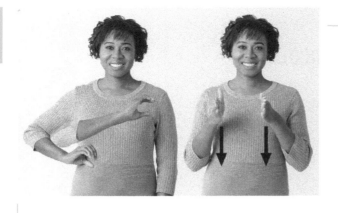

CHRISTIAN

This sign is a combination of CHRIST and PERSON (page 217). Your dominant hand first signs CHRIST with the hand in a C handshape by placing it on your nondominant shoulder. Then, bring your hand down to touch at your waist on the nondominant side. Sign PERSON with both hands in flat open handshapes, palms facing each other but several inches apart. Bring your hands straight down several inches while maintaining the handshapes and palm orientation.

CHRISTMAS

Make a C handshape with your dominant hand, palm facing down. Flip the wrist while moving the hand upward so that the palm faces inward.

TIP: There are multiple variations and signing styles for this sign. Refer to your local Deaf community to learn other variations.

CHURCH

Make a fist with your nondominant hand, palm facing down, and make a C handshape with your dominant hand, palm facing outward. Tap the thumb of your dominant hand on the back of your nondominant hand two times.

CITY/TOWN

With both hands in flat open handshapes, palms facing each other and fingertips together, twist your palms alternately while maintaining contact at the fingertips.

CLEAN/NICE

Hold out your nondominant hand in a flat hand-shape, palm facing up. With your dominant hand, also in a flat handshape, wipe the palm across the palm of your nondominant hand, moving away from the body.

TIP: Think of wiping a whiteboard clean.

CLICK

Hold your dominant hand up in front of your body in a modified 5 handshape, palm facing outward, with the middle finger extended forward. Tap the space in front of you with your middle finger.

CLOGGED (See: Stuck/Trapped/Clogged, page 265)

CLOSE-BY

Make an F handshape with your dominant hand, palm facing inward. Brush the tip of your pinched index finger and thumb off the tip of your nose in a downward direction. As you do so, hold your mouth in a tight "ooo" shape.

CLOSED (See: Open/Closed, page 211)

CLOTHES/DRESS

With both hands in 5 handshapes, palms facing inward, touch your hands to your shoulders and move them downward two times.

If you make just one long downward movement, it becomes the sign for DRESS.

CLOUDS/STORM

With both hands in front of your face in claw handshapes, palms facing each other, make alternating circles in the air with both hands.

If you move the hands more intently with a cautionary facial expression, you can communicate STORM.

COAT/JACKET

With both hands in A handshapes, palms facing inward and thumbs pointed upward, touch your thumbs to your shoulders and move the hands downward.

TIP: Think of the movement of pulling on a coat or jacket.

COFFEE

With both hands in S handshapes, palms facing inward or to the side and your dominant hand resting on top of your nondominant hand, move your dominant hand in a counterclockwise circle two times.

TIP: Imagine grinding coffee beans.

COLD (TEMPERATURE)

With both hands in S handshapes held out in front of your body, palms facing each other, shake your hands side to side as if you were shivering.

TIP: When making this sign, use body language and a facial expression that demonstrates what you look like when you feel cold.

x2

COLD (ILLNESS)

With your dominant hand, make a double pinching downward movement from the tip of your nose with the thumb and index finger.

TIP: Think of wiping your nose with a small tissue.

COLLEGE

With both hands in 5 handshapes, hold your nondominant hand in front of you, palm facing up. Press the flat palm of your dominant hand onto the other palm, then move it upward in a slight circular motion, away from the nondominant hand.

COLOR/COLORFUL

Make a 5 handshape with your dominant hand, palm facing inward, then touch your fingertips to your chin and wiggle your fingers.

If you make this sign with both hands, touching the chin alternately, it becomes the sign for COLORFUL.

COME

With both hands in 1 handshapes, palms facing up, lift both hands up toward your body, ending with your palms facing inward.

TIP: To communicate GO (page 43), palms face forward and move your fingers away from your body instead of toward you.

COMMITMENT (See: Promise/Commitment, page 225)

x2

COMMUTE

Make a thumbs-up handshape with your dominant hand in front of your body and move it side to side several times.

TIP: Think of repeatedly traveling the path between two places.

COMPETE/COMPETITOR/ATHLETE/RACE

With both hands in A handshapes, thumbs pointed upward, bring your fists together, palms facing each other. Twist your fists alternately, keeping the knuckles together.

If you add the PERSON sign (page 217) at the end of this sign, you can indicate the nouns COMPETITOR or ATHLETE. Sign PERSON with both hands in flat open handshapes, palms facing each other but several inches apart. Bring your hands straight down several inches while maintaining the handshapes and palm orientation.

COMPLAIN

Make a loose C handshape with your dominant hand and knock your fingertips against the upper center of your chest two or more times.

TIP: Intensity or repeated complaints can be indicated with more knocking movements and an emphatic facial expression.

COMPUTER

Make a C handshape with your dominant hand, palm facing to the side. Hold your nondominant arm in front of your body and tap along it with your dominant hand in an upward arching motion two or three times.

TIP: There are multiple signs for COMPUTER. Defer to your local Deaf community.

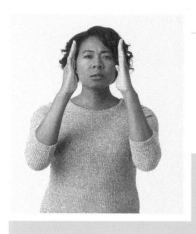

CONCENTRATE/FOCUS

With both hands in flat handshapes, touch them to the sides of your head and move them forward, away from the face, one or more times.

TIP: Think of blocking out any distractions and focusing your attention on only what is right in front of you.

CONCERN

With both hands in 5 handshapes, palms facing inward and the middle fingers extended forward, tap the middle fingers alternately to your upper chest.

TIP: Show a concerned expression with this sign.

CONFIDENCE/CONFIDENT (See: Brave/Confident/Healthy, page 62)

x2

CONFUSED

With both hands in claw handshapes near the forehead, palms facing each other, make rotating, circular motions with both hands while keeping the palms facing each other.

TIP: People often point to the side of the forehead before they do this sign, almost like communicating "brain fog."

CONTINUE

With both hands in A handshapes, palms facing down, touch the thumbs to each other and move the hands forward, away from the body.

TIP: You can emphasize this sign by moving your hands even further forward, repeating the forward motion, or making a straining facial expression.

CONTROL/MANAGE/MANAGER/RULER

With both hands in X handshapes, palms facing each other but not touching, move the hands forward and back alternately two times.

Add the PERSON sign (page 217) at the end to indicate the noun MANAGER or RULER. Sign PERSON with both hands in flat open handshapes, palms facing each other but several inches apart. Bring your hands straight down several inches while maintaining the handshapes and palm orientation.

COOK/PANCAKES

Hold out your nondominant hand in a flat open handshape, palm facing up. With your dominant hand also in a flat handshape, clap each side of the hand down on your nondominant hand, as if cooking something on both sides. Repeat this flipping motion for the full sign.

If you make a bigger flipping movement, this becomes the sign for PANCAKES.

COOKIE

Hold out your nondominant hand in a 5 hand-shape, palm facing up. With your dominant hand in a claw handshape, touch the palm of your non-dominant hand with your fingertips and twist the hand two times.

TIP: Imagine your hand in the claw handshape is a cookie cutter.

COOL (STYLISH)

Make a 5 handshape with your dominant hand, palm facing to the side, then touch the tip of your thumb to your chest and wiggle your fingers.

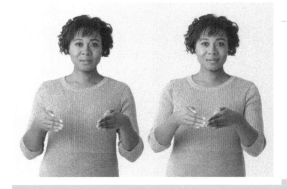

CORNER

With both hands in flat B handshapes and positioned horizontally, bring the fingertips of both hands together to form a right angle, or corner, with your hands.

TIP: You're showing two lines meeting together in a point: a corner.

CORRECT (See: Right [correct/accurate], page 233)

COST (See: Charge/Cost/Fee/Fine/Price/Tax, page 73)

COUCH

This sign is a combination of SIT (page 72) and showing the shape of a couch. First, sign SIT with both hands in U handshapes (the handshape is often bent on the dominant hand), palms down. Tap your dominant fingers on top of your nondominant fingers one time. Show the shape of a couch with both hands in C handshapes, palms facing down, the sides of your hands touching. Pull both hands away from each other in opposite directions.

COUGH

Make a fist with your dominant hand and knock your fist against your upper chest two or more times.

TIP: Think of trying to clear your lungs of an obstruction.

COUNSEL (See: Advice/Counsel, page 27)

COUNT

Hold out your nondominant hand in a flat handshape, palm facing up. With your dominant hand in an F handshape, touch the thumb and index fingers to the palm of your nondominant hand and make a forward sliding movement two or more times.

TIP: Think of counting a handful of coins, one at a time.

COUNTRY

Hold your nondominant arm up with your hand relaxed near your shoulder. Make a flat handshape with your dominant hand and touch the palm to your nondominant elbow, rubbing it in a circular motion two times.

COUSIN (MALE/FEMALE/NEUTRAL)

Make a C handshape with your dominant hand near the side of your face, palm facing inward, and wiggle the hand two times.

TIP: You can indicate a male cousin by making this sign by the upper part of your face. You can indicate a female cousin by making the sign by the lower part of your face. To make the sign gender neutral, sign it by the center of your face.

COW

Make a Y handshape with your dominant hand, palm facing outward, and touch your thumb to the side of your forehead. Twist the hand forward two times, keeping the thumb in place.

TIP: Imagine a cow's horn on the side of your head.

CPR Fingerspell the letters C-P-R with your dominant hand.

CRACKERS (See: Passover/Crackers, page 214)

CRAZY

Make a claw handshape with your dominant hand and hold it to the side of your face, a few inches away. Make a twisting movement from the wrist two times.

CREATE/CREATIVE/INVENT

Make a 4 handshape with your dominant hand, palm facing to the side, and touch your index finger to the side of your forehead before moving the hand outward, away from the body.

If you make a double movement, it becomes the adjective CREATIVE.

TIP: You can also do this sign with two hands for emphasis.

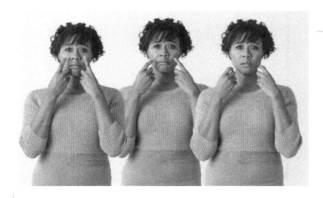

CRY

With both hands in 1 hand-shapes, palms facing inward, touch your fingertips to your cheeks just under the eyes. Drag your index fingers down your cheeks like tears falling.

CULTURE

Hold out your nondominant hand in a 1 handshape, palm facing outward. With the fingertips of your dominant hand in a flat O handshape, touch the index finger of your nondominant hand and rotate around it while making a C handshape, then close into a flat O handshape again.

TIP: This sign can also be done with a C handshape instead of a flat O.

CUP/GLASS/CAN

Hold out your nondominant hand in a 5 handshape, palm facing up. With your dominant hand in a C handshape, touch the bottom of your hand to the open palm of your nondominant hand. Repeat this motion two times.

TIP: Think of tapping the bottom of a glass on a tabletop.

CURIOUS

With your dominant hand, pinch a bit of the skin on the front of your neck with the thumb and index finger and twist the hand slightly a couple of times.

CUSHION (See: Pillow/Cushion, page 220)

CUTE

Make a U handshape with your dominant hand, palm facing inward, and touch your fingertips to the tip of your chin, moving them downward as they fold into an A handshape.

TIP: This movement can also be repeated two times.

DAD/FATHER

Make a 5 handshape with your dominant hand, palm facing to the side, and touch the tip of the thumb to your forehead or tap it to your forehead slightly two times.

TIP: The upper part of the face is the reference point for male referents.

DAILY (See: Everyday/Daily, page 115)

DAIRY (See: Milk/Dairy, page 192)

DANCE

Hold out your nondominant hand in a flat open handshape, palm facing up. Make a V handshape with your dominant hand, fingertips pointing down toward the center of your nondominant palm. With your dominant hand above but not touching the palm, move your fingers side to side by twisting your wrist.

TIP: Imagine feet gliding across a dance floor.

DANGER/HAZARD

Hold your nondominant hand in either a fist or a flat handshape, palm facing inward. Make an A handshape with your dominant hand and brush the thumb upward against the back of your nondominant fist two times.

TIP: Use a more intense expression for more emphasis.

DARK

With both hands in flat handshapes, palms facing inward at eye level, bring both hands downward, crossing them as they come down.

TIP: Think of curtains or a cover coming down.

DAUGHTER

Make flat B handshapes with both hands. Position your nondominant hand in front of the body, palm facing up, as if holding a baby. With the fingers of your dominant hand, touch the side of the face near the chin (female reference point), then drop the hand down until it rests in the crook of your nondominant elbow with the palm facing up.

DAY

Hold your nondominant arm in front of your body, palm facing down. Make a 1 handshape with your dominant hand and rest the elbow on top of the fingers of your nondominant hand with your index finger pointing straight up. Drop your dominant arm down to the side to land on top of your nondominant arm.

TIP: You can incorporate numbers (up to 9) into this sign to show how many days.

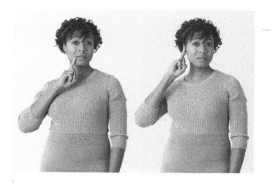

DEAF

Make a 1 handshape with your dominant hand, palm facing outward, and touch your index finger to the side of your chin. Move the finger away from your chin and touch the back of the jaw.

TIP: You will also see this signed with the finger starting at the back of the jaw and ending on the chin.

DEBT (See: Bill/Debt/Due/Owe, page 54)

DECIDE/DECISION

With both hands in F handshapes, palms facing each other in front of the body, make a downward movement with both hands at the same time.

DEER

With both hands in 5 handshapes, touch your thumbs to each side of your forehead and move them upward and outward.

TIP: This sign resembles antlers.

DENTIST

Make an X handshape with your dominant hand and tap your fingernail to your teeth two times.

This sign can also be done with an A handshape on the cheek.

DEPART (See: Leave [depart], page 178)

DEPARTMENT

With both hands in D handshapes, palms facing outward and your index fingers touching each other, rotate the hands away from each other and circle forward until the hands meet again at the pinkies with the palms now facing inward.

TIP: This is the same sign as FAMILY (page 120), except it uses a D handshape instead of an F.

DEPEND/RELY-ON

With both hands in 1 handshapes in front of the body, palms facing down, cross your index fingers and push them downward. Repeat the movement one or more times.

DEPRESSED

With both hands in 5 handshapes and the middle fingers extended forward, touch the middle fingers to each respective side of the body, just inside the shoulder blades. Slide both hands downward.

TIP: Think of the downward movement representing "feeling down."

DESCRIBE/DIRECTIONS/EXPLAIN/ INSTRUCTIONS

With both hands in F handshapes in front of the body, palms facing each other but not touching, move the hands forward and back alternately.

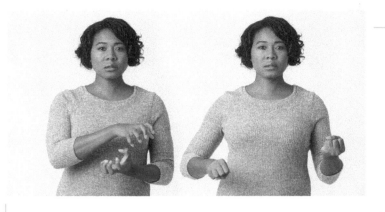

DESTROY

With both hands in 5 or claw handshapes in front of the body, position one above the other, palms facing each other. Cross your hands past each other, then as you uncross them to the starting position, change your handshapes into fists. This sign can be repeated to show ongoing or repeated destruction.

TIP: Think of the movement of crumpling and ripping something apart.

DIFFERENT

With both hands in 1 handshapes, palms facing outward, hold up both index fingers and form an X by crossing them. Uncross them as your hands move away from each other and out to the sides.

DIMPLES (See: Candy/Dimples, page 69)

DINNER/SUPPER

This sign is a combination of EAT (page 110) and NIGHT (page 204). First, sign EAT with a flat O handshape brought to your lips once, and then quickly sign NIGHT: Hold your nondominant arm in front of the body horizontally in a flat B handshape. Make a bent B handshape with your dominant hand. Place the wrist of your dominant hand on top of your nondominant hand, with the fingertips pointing toward the floor.

DIRECTIONS (See: Describe/Directions/Explain/Instructions, page 97)

DIRTY

Make a 5 handshape with your dominant hand, palm facing down, touch the back of your hand below your chin, and wiggle your fingers.

TIP: Think of dirt in a beard.

DISAPPOINTED/MISS-YOU

Make a 1 handshape with your dominant hand, palm facing inward, and hold the tip of your index finger to your chin while making a disappointed expression.

The sign for MISS-YOU is the same, but your face takes on a more sorrowful expression.

DISCIPLINE (See: Punish/Discipline, page 226)

DISCONNECT/BREAK-UP

With both hands in F handshapes, interlock your fingers as if they were links of a chain, then pull them apart and out to the sides.

TIP: Imagine links of a chain breaking apart.

DISH/PLATE

With both hands in open 8 or modified C handshapes, palms facing each other, hold your hands in front of your body with just your thumbs and index fingers extended.

TIP: This is technically a classifier. It looks like the shape of a plate.

DIVORCED (See: Married/Divorced, page 188)

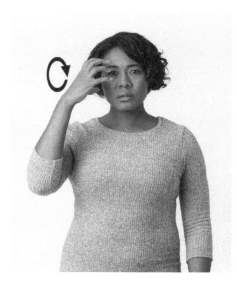

DIZZY

Make a claw handshape and hold it by the side of your forehead, palm facing inward, making a circular motion with your hand.

TIP: Imagine things jumbling around in your skull. Use a confused expression while making this sign.

DOCTOR

Hold out your nondominant hand in a flat handshape, palm facing up. Make a flat bent handshape with your dominant hand and touch the tips of your fingers to your nondominant wrist two times.

DOG

Snap the fingers of your dominant hand as you would to call a dog to come to you.

TIP: Another way to sign DOG is by patting your upper leg, which is another common way to call a dog to come.

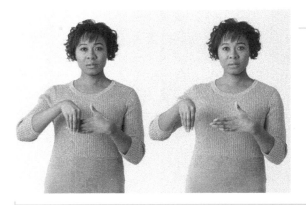

DOLLAR

Hold out your nondominant hand in a flat handshape, palm facing inward. Clasp the fingers of your nondominant hand with the opposite hand as you move your dominant hand out to the side.

TIP: Imagine sliding a money clip off a stack of bills.

DON'T-CARE

With your dominant hand, pinch all of your fingers together and touch them to the tip of your nose. Point them away from your face as you open your fingers into a 5 handshape.

DON'T-HAVE (See: Have/Don't-Have, page 153)

DON'T-KNOW

Make a flat open handshape with your dominant hand, touch the fingers to the side of your forehead, and then twist your hand away from your head so that your palm is now facing outward.

TIP: This movement is made in the opposite direction from the sign for KNOW (page 174).

DON'T-LIKE

Make a 5 handshape against your chest with your dominant hand, palm facing inward. Make a pulling motion with your hand, as if pulling a string, and as you pull, bring your thumb and middle fingers together (this is the sign for LIKE). Next, reverse your wrist so that your palm faces outward and flick your middle finger off your thumb, as if you were flicking a piece of lint off your shirt.

DON'T-MIND

Make a 1 handshape with your dominant hand and touch your index finger to the tip of your nose, then point your index finger away from the body while moving your hand away from your face.

TIP: If you make this sign with a Y/N? expression (page 7) on your face, you are asking DO YOU MIND? instead of stating I DON'T MIND.

DON'T-UNDERSTAND (See: Understand/Don't-Understand, page 291)

DON'T-WANT (See: Want/Don't-Want, page 298)

DOOR

With both hands in B hand-shapes, palms facing outward and hands positioned side by side in front of your body, turn the wrist of your dominant hand toward you like opening a door.

TIP: Imagine that your hands are closed French doors and open just the door on the dominant side.

DOUBT

Make a V handshape with your dominant hand at eye level, palm facing inward. Bend the fingers two times.

DOWNLOAD/UPLOAD/INSTALL

With both hands in V handshapes near the shoulders, palms facing each other, position your dominant hand just above your nondominant hand. Drag the hands down, and as you reach the bottom of the movement, bend your fingers into the bent V handshape.

DREAM

Make a 1 handshape with your dominant hand and touch the index finger to the side of your forehead, then bend it repeatedly into an X handshape as you move it away from your head.

DRESS (See: Clothes/Dress, page 78)

DRINK

Make a C handshape in front of your mouth with your dominant hand, palm facing to the side, and pantomime the movement of taking a drink from a cup.

TIP: If you make this sign with an A or Y handshape, you are implying that the drink is alcoholic.

DRIVE (See: Car/Drive, page 70)

DRY

Make a 1 handshape with your dominant hand, palm facing down, and touch the side of the index finger to your chin. Move it across the chin and out to the side while shifting into an X handshape.

TIP: Imagine wiping moisture off your chin so that it is dry.

DUE (See: Bill/Debt/Due/Owe, page 54)

DURING/WHILE

With both hands in 1 handshapes, palms facing down, index fingers side by side, hold your hands close to the body then slide the fingers outward, away from the body, while keeping the fingers parallel with each other.

TIP: Think of two things happening simultaneously on a timeline.

DUTY (See: Responsible/Duty/Obligation/Chore, page 232)

EARLY

Hold out your nondominant hand in either a flat handshape or a fist, palm facing down. With your dominant hand in a 5 handshape, touch your middle fingertip to the back of the nondominant hand and trace a line forward over the wrist.

TIP: Be careful not to get this sign mixed up with BARE/NUDE, which is made by sliding the dominant hand to the side toward the fingertips rather than forward.

EARN

Hold out your nondominant hand in a flat handshape, palm facing up. Rest your dominant hand in an open fist on top of your nondominant palm and pull your dominant hand toward you as you close the hand into a fist.

TIP: Think of gathering coins that are piled in your palm.

EARTH

Make an S handshape with your nondominant hand and make an open 8 handshape with your dominant hand. Place the tips of your dominant middle finger and thumb on the back of your nondominant hand and wiggle the hand forward and back.

EARTHQUAKE

First, sign EARTH: Make an S handshape with your nondominant hand and make an open 8 handshape with your dominant hand. Place the tips of your dominant middle finger and thumb on the back of your nondominant hand and wiggle the hand forward and back. Then, immediately shift both hands into fists with the palms facing down. Jerk your hands quickly side to side.

TIP: Imagine the earth being shaken.

EAST

Hold up your dominant hand in an E handshape and slide it to the right.

EASTER

With both hands in E handshapes, palms facing each other, twist your wrists so that your palms shift forward two times.

EASY (See: Almost/Easy, page 33)

EAT/FOOD/FEAST

Bring your dominant hand in a flat O handshape directly to your lips. If you make a repeated tapping movement on the lips, this becomes the noun FOOD.

TIP: If you use both hands in large movements, you are communicating FEAST.

EGG

With both hands in U handshapes, stack the fingers of one hand on the fingers of the other, then have them both collapse downward in either 1 or 2 movements.

TIP: This sign looks somewhat like the action of cracking an egg.

ELEMENTARY

Hold up your nondominant hand in a flat handshape, palm facing down. Make an E handshape with your dominant hand, palm facing outward, and rock it side to side under the palm of your nondominant hand.

ELEPHANT

Make a flat handshape with your dominant hand, palm facing down, then touch the tip of your fingers to your nose and slide the hand downward and outward.

TIP: The movement of this sign looks like the curve of an elephant's trunk.

EMAIL/SEND-AN-EMAIL

Make a C handshape with your nondominant hand, palm facing to the side, and make a 1 handshape (or a flat bent handshape) with your dominant hand. Point the index finger of your dominant hand toward your body, then swipe it forward two times in the open space of your nondominant hand.

If you make just one movement instead of two, you are communicating SEND-AN-EMAIL.

EMBARRASSED

With both hands in 5 handshapes, hold both palms close to the cheeks and alternately move them upward in circular movements.

TIP: Think of red flushed cheeks from feeling embarrassed. There are several other ways to sign this word. Defer to your local Deaf community.

EMERGENCY

Hold up an E handshape with your dominant hand, palm facing outward, and shake your hand side to side a few times.

TIP: Think of waving to get someone's attention due to an urgent situation.

END

With both hands in flat handshapes, hold your nondominant hand horizontally in front of your body, palm facing inward. With your dominant hand facing to the side, move the hand straight downward at the end of the fingertips.

ENGAGED (TO BE MARRIED)

Hold up your nondominant hand in a flat handshape, palm facing down. With your dominant hand in an E handshape, make a circular motion above your nondominant hand before landing it on the ring finger.

ENJOY

With both hands in flat open handshapes, palms facing inward, place your dominant hand on your chest and your nondominant hand on your stomach. Circle your hands, with your dominant hand circling clockwise and your nondominant hand circling counterclockwise.

ENVISION (See: Visualize/Vision/Envision/Imagine, page 296)

EQUAL/FAIR

Hold up both hands in flat bent handshapes, palms facing each other, and tap the tips of the fingers together.

TIP: Think of the scales of justice being balanced perfectly.

ESCAPE/RUN-AWAY

Hold out your nondominant hand in a 5 handshape, palm facing down. Make a 1 handshape with your dominant hand, poke the index finger up through the space between the index and middle fingers of your nondominant hand, and quickly move it away to the side.

TIP: Think of the finger as an escapee running away.

EUROPE

Make an E handshape with your dominant hand, palm facing to the side, and draw a circle with it near the side of your forehead.

EVENING (See: Night/Evening, page 204)

EVENT (See: Excited/Thrilled/Event, page 115)

EVERYDAY/DAILY

Make an A handshape with your dominant hand and touch the back of your fingers to your jawline, then slide the hand forward two times.

TIP: This sign is similar to the sign for TOMORROW (page 284).

EXAM (See: Test/Exam, page 277)

EXCITED/THRILLED/EVENT

With both hands in 5 handshapes, palms facing inward and the middle finger extended forward, alternately brush your middle fingers up the sides of your chest in a circular motion two times. If you move both hands upward simultaneously one time, you are communicating THRILLED or EVENT.

TIP: Think of lots of happy feelings jumping around in your body.

EXCUSE/FORGIVE

With both hands in flat handshapes, brush the fingertips of your dominant hand past the fingertips of your nondominant hand a couple of times.

TIP: If you make just one movement, it means the act has been completed, or FORGIVEN and EXCUSED.

EXERCISE/WORKOUT/GYM

With both hands in fists next to your shoulders, palms facing outward, move both arms up and down.

TIP: Think of the action of lifting weights.

EXHAUSTED (See: Tired/Exhausted, page 283)

EXPECT/HOPE

With both hands in flat bent handshapes next to the side of your head, palms facing each other, wave your fingers up and down two times.

EXPENSIVE

Hold out your nondominant hand in a flat handshape, palm facing up. With your dominant hand in a flat O handshape, make a gesture that looks like you are picking something up from the palm of the other hand and throwing it off to the side.

TIP: Think of how expensive items can sometimes feel like you are throwing money away.

EXPERIENCE

With your dominant hand against your cheek, fingers open, move your fingers down the side of your cheek two times while closing them together at the end of each downward movement.

EXPLAIN (See: Describe/Directions/Explain/Instructions, page 97)

FACE (See: Looks/Looks-Like/Face, page 183)

FACIAL-EXPRESSION

Make X handshapes with both hands and position them next to each side of the face, palms facing your face, and move them up and down a couple of times.

TIP: Think of holding puppet strings connected to your face that control your expressions.

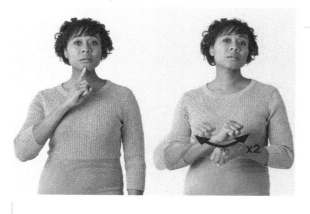

FACT/SURE-ENOUGH/ REAL-DEAL/TRUE-BIZ

This sign is a combination of TRUE (page 229) and WORK (page 312). Your dominant hand first signs TRUE with the hand in a 1 handshape, palm facing to the side. Touch the side of your index finger to your chin and mouth, moving the finger slightly upward and outward in an arch.

For WORK, with both hands in S handshapes, palms facing down, tap the wrist of your dominant hand on the wrist of your nondominant hand two times.

TIP: TRUE-BIZ is considered an ASL idiom, or figure of speech. It can be used to state that something is a fact and also to convey statements such as SURE ENOUGH, I REALLY MEAN IT, or IT'S REALLY TRUE.

FAIL

Hold up your nondominant hand in an open handshape. With your dominant hand in a K handshape, slide the hand across the palm of your nondominant hand, moving away from the body.

FAIR (See: Equal/Fair, page 114)

FAKE (See: False/Fake, page 120)

FALL (SEASON)

Hold up your nondominant arm, hand relaxed. With your dominant hand in a B handshape, brush the side of the hand two times past your nondominant elbow.

TIP: The brushing motion of the dominant hand is like the leaves falling off the "branch" of your nondominant arm.

FALSE/FAKE

Make a 1 handshape with your dominant hand and brush the side of your index finger across the tip of the nose.

FAMILY

With both hands in F handshapes, palms facing outward and the tips of your thumbs and index fingers pinched together in front of your body, rotate your hands around until your pinky fingers touch and your palms are facing inward.

FAMOUS (See: Success/Famous, page 266)

F

FANCY/FORMAL/MANNERS/POLITE

Make a 5 handshape with your dominant hand, palm facing to the side, and touch the tip of the thumb to the center of the chest a couple of times while moving it in an upward circular motion.

    Smaller circular motions turn this sign into the concepts MANNERS and POLITE.

FAR

With both hands held together in front of the body in A handshapes, palms facing each other, move the dominant fist forward and slightly upward while keeping the nondominant fist in place.

TIP: Think of one hand being far ahead of the other one.

FARM/FARMER/RANCH/RANCHER

Make a 5 handshape with your dominant hand and touch the tip of the thumb to the opposite side of the jaw, sliding the hand to the other side of the jaw while keeping the thumb in contact with the face.

You can add the PERSON sign (page 217) after the sign for FARM to communicate FARMER. Sign PERSON with both hands in flat open handshapes, palms facing each other but several inches apart. Bring your hands straight down several inches while maintaining the handshapes and palm orientation.

You can also change the handshape to an R to indicate RANCH/RANCHER.

FAST

Make L handshapes with both hands, palms facing each other. Position your dominant hand slightly in front of your nondominant hand. Curl your index fingers as if pulling a trigger, and make your hands pop up slightly with this motion.

FATHER (See: Dad/Father, page 92)

FATHER-IN-LAW

This sign is a combination of DAD (page 92) and LAW (page 177). You first sign DAD with your dominant hand in the 5 handshape, palm facing to the side. Touch the tip of the thumb to your forehead or tap it to your forehead slightly two times. To sign LAW, hold your nondominant hand in a flat handshape, palm facing up or to the side. Make an L handshape with your dominant hand, palm facing to the side, and tap your dominant palm on the upper portion of your nondominant palm. Move your dominant hand down, and then tap your dominant palm on the bottom portion of your nondominant palm.

FAULT (See: Accuse/Blame/Fault, page 26)

FAVORITE/PREFER

Make a 5 handshape with your dominant hand and extend the middle finger forward. Tap the tip of your middle finger to your chin two times.

FEAST (See: Eat/Food/Feast, page 110)

FEE (See: Charge/Cost/Fee/Fine/Price/Tax, page 73)

FEEL

Make a 5 handshape with your dominant hand and extend the middle finger forward. Touch the extended middle finger to the center of your chest and make two upward stroking movements.

FEEL-SORRY-FOR (See: Pity/Mercy/Feel-Sorry-For, page 220)

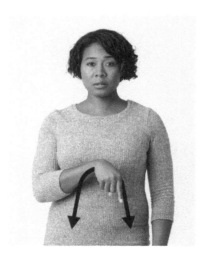

FEET

Make a 1 handshape with your dominant hand and make downward pointing motions in the direction of each foot.

TIP: You do not need to lean down to get closer to your feet for this sign.

FIANCÉ/ FIANCÉE

Hold out your nondominant hand in a flat hand-shape, palm facing down. Make an F handshape with your dominant hand and circle it slightly above the ring finger of your nondominant hand before landing directly on the ring finger.

FIELD (See: Area/Field/Ground, page 40)

FIGURE-OUT (See: Worse/Figure-Out, page 313)

FILE

With both hands in flat open hand-shapes, position the nondominant hand vertically, palm facing to the side, and position the dominant hand horizontally, palm facing inward. Slide your dominant hand between the middle and ring fingers of your nondominant hand.

TIP: Imagine that your nondominant hand is a file cabinet and each finger represents a divider.

FINAL (See: Last/Final, page 175)

FINALLY/ AT-LAST

Touch both index fingertips to your chin, palms facing inward, then reverse the palms outward while moving your hands away from the body and out to the sides of your face.

TIP: This sign has a nonmanual marker that accompanies it; quietly say "PAH!" as you move your fingers outward.

FIND/PICK

Make a 5 handshape with your dominant hand, palm facing down, and pinch your fingers into an F handshape as you pull your hand upward.

TIP: Think of the gesture of picking a very small weed out of the ground.

FINE (FEELING)/OKAY

Make a 5 handshape with your dominant hand, palm facing to the side. Bring your thumb to your chest and tap it a couple of times. You can also do one exaggerated tap to say this with an attitude.

FINE (PAYMENT) (See: Charge/Cost/Fee/Fine/Price/Tax, page 73)

FINGERSPELL/SPELL

Hold your dominant hand in a 5 handshape in front of the shoulder area of the dominant side of your body, palm facing outward, and wiggle your fingers as you slide the hand out to the side.

One sliding movement indicates the verbs SPELL or FINGERSPELL, and two sliding movements indicate the nouns SPELLING or FINGERSPELLING.

FINISHED/ ALL-DONE

With both hands in front of the body in 5 handshapes, palms facing inward, shake both hands briskly, as if trying to air-dry wet hands.

FIRE

With both hands in 5 handshapes, palms facing inward, move your hands alternately in a circular motion while wiggling the fingers.

TIP: You can communicate how big or intense a fire is based on how big you sign this and how intense your movements and facial expressions are.

FIREFIGHTER

Make a B handshape with your dominant hand, palm facing outward. Tap the back of your hand to your forehead.

TIP: This tapping motion indicates the front of a firefighter's helmet.

FIRST

Make a thumbs-up with your nondominant hand. With your dominant hand in a 1 handshape, tap the tip of your index finger to the tip of your nondominant thumb.

TIP: Think of your thumb being the first finger on the hand.

FISH

Make a flat open handshape with your dominant hand and position it horizontally, palm facing to the side. Shake your hand slightly while moving it forward quickly.

TIP: Imagine the movement of a fish swimming through the water.

FIX/REPAIR

With both hands in flat O handshapes, brush the tops of the fingertips of both hands past each other two times.

FLAG

Make a flat handshape with your dominant hand and position it horizontally, palm facing to the side. Set the elbow of your dominant hand on the back of your nondominant hand and wave your dominant hand back and forth two times.

TIP: Think of a flag blowing in a breeze.

FLOWER

Make a flat O handshape with your dominant hand and touch the tips of the fingers to each side of the nose.

TIP: Think of sniffing flowers.

FLY (See: Airplane/Fly, page 30)

FOCUS (See: Concentrate/Focus, page 83)

FOG (See: Smoke/Fog, page 249)

FOLLOW/CHASE

With both hands in thumbs-up handshapes, put one fist in front of the other, then move both hands forward.

If you move the back fist in a circular movement throughout, this sign becomes CHASE.

FOOD (See: Eat/Food/Feast, page 110)

FOOTBALL

With both hands in 5 handshapes, palms facing each other, bring your hands together and interlock your fingers. Repeat this movement two times.

TIP: Imagine a line of players from two opposing teams crashing together in a tackle.

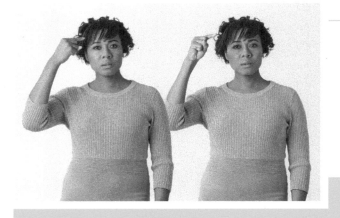

FOR/WHAT-FOR?

Make a 1 handshape with your dominant hand and touch your index fingertip to your temple, then twist your wrist forward once.

TIP: If you repeat the movement two times with a WH? expression (page 7), you are asking WHAT-FOR?

FORCE

Hold out your dominant hand in a C handshape, palm facing inward, then turn the palm to face outward and slightly downward.

TIP: Think of turning something away from you forcefully.

FOREST (See: Tree/Forest, page 288)

FORGET

Make a flat handshape with your dominant hand and touch your fingertips to the opposite side of your forehead, dragging them across the head as they close into an A handshape.

TIP: Imagine your forehead as a whiteboard and use your fingers to wipe it clean.

FORGIVE (See: Excuse/Forgive, page 116)

FORK

Hold out your nondominant hand in a flat handshape, palm facing up. With your dominant hand in a V handshape, tap the tips of your fingers to the palm of your nondominant hand two times.

TIP: Think of poking the prongs of a fork into a steak.

FORMAL (See: Fancy/Formal/Manners/Polite, page 121)

FRACTURE (See: Break [fracture], page 62)

FREE/FREEDOM

With both hands in fists, cross your wrists, palms facing inward, then uncross them as you turn the palms outward.

    If you do this sign with F handshapes, it becomes the sign for FREE, as in no cost.

FREEZE/FREEZER/ICE

With both hands in 5 handshapes, palms facing down or outward, stiffen and bend the fingers as you pull your hands closer to your body.

    If you stiffen and bend the fingers two times, it becomes the sign for FREEZER. If you sign WATER (page 300) before this sign, making a W handshape with your dominant hand and tapping the side of your index finger to the front of your chin/mouth area two times, it becomes the sign for ICE.

FRENCH-FRIES/TATER-TOTS

Make an F handshape with your dominant hand, palm facing outward, and drop your hand slightly forward two times.

If you do this sign with a T handshape, it becomes TATER-TOTS.

FREQUENTLY (See: Often/Frequently, page 210)

FRESH (See: New/Fresh, page 203)

FRIEND/ BEST-FRIEND

With both hands in X handshapes, the palm of your nondominant hand facing up and the palm of your dominant hand facing down, hook your index fingers together briefly and then flip your hands so that your dominant hand is now facing up and the nondominant hand is facing down, again hooking your index fingers together briefly.

If you hook your index fingers together and move both hands forward firmly, rather than reversing positions, you are communicating CLOSE or BEST-FRIEND.

FRIENDLY

Hold both hands in 5 handshapes next to the cheeks and move the hands backward and out to the side while wiggling the fingers.

TIP: This can also be used to communicate a pleasant or charismatic disposition.

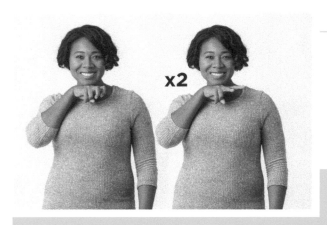

x2

FROG

Hold your dominant hand under your chin, palm facing down, and flick a V handshape two times from the thumb.

TIP: Think of the expanding and contracting of a frog's chin as it croaks.

FROM

With both hands in 1 handshapes, point your dominant index finger at your nondominant index finger and pull the dominant hand toward your body as the index finger changes into an X handshape.

FRUIT

Make an F handshape with your dominant hand and touch the pinched index finger and thumb to the side of your cheek, twisting your hand two times.

FRUSTRATED

Make a B handshape with your dominant hand and hit the tip of your chin with the back of your hand one or more times.

FULL

Make an S handshape with your nondominant hand, palm facing to the side, and make a flat hand-shape with your dominant hand, palm facing down. Slide the palm of your dominant hand across the top of the S handshape.

FUN

With both hands in U handshapes, position your nondominant hand with the palm facing down. Touch the tips of your two dominant fingers to the tip of your nose, then flip the palm downward and move the two fingers so they land on the back of your two nondominant fingers.

FUNERAL

With both hands in V handshapes, palms facing outward, position your dominant hand in front of your nondominant hand. They should not touch. Slide the hands away from your body two times.

TIP: This sign is typically done with a somber facial expression.

FUNNY

Make a U handshape with your dominant hand and brush the two fingertips up and down the tip of your nose two times.

FUTURE/SOMEDAY

Make a flat handshape with your dominant hand and position your palm at the side of your head, then move the hand forward.

TIP: You can indicate something being further into the future by moving the hand further forward while squinting your eyes, as if looking at something far away.

GAME

With both hands in A handshapes, palms facing inward, tap the knuckles of both hands together two times.

GASOLINE

Hold out your nondominant hand in a fist, palm facing to the side, and tap the tip of your dominant thumb into the tight space made by the closed fist.

TIP: Think of inserting a gas nozzle into a vehicle.

GAY

Make a G handshape with your dominant hand and touch the thumb and index fingertips to the bottom of your chin.

TIP: This word is also commonly fingerspelled.

GET/RECEIVE/ACQUIRE

With both hands in 5 handshapes, reach both hands outward, one above the other, and pull both hands back while closing them into fists.

TIP: Think of reaching out and grabbing something you want to get.

GET-IN

Make a C handshape with your nondominant hand, palm facing to the side, and make a bent V handshape with your dominant hand. Imagine that both fingers are legs and your C hand is a vehicle. "Seat" the fingers of your dominant hand by hooking them onto the thumb of your nondominant hand.

GET-OUT

This is signed the same way as GET-IN, except you unhook the fingers of your dominant hand from your nondominant thumb to mimic a person getting out of a vehicle.

GIRL

Make an A handshape with your dominant hand and brush the tip of the thumb down the dominant side of your jawline.

TIP: Think of a curl of hair framing the chin.

GIRLFRIEND

This sign is a combination of GIRL and FRIEND (page 135). Your dominant hand first signs GIRL with an A handshape, brushing the tip of the thumb down the dominant side of your jawline. For FRIEND, with both hands in X handshapes, the palm of your nondominant hand facing up and the palm of your dominant hand facing down, hook your index fingers together briefly and then flip your hands so that your dominant hand is now facing up and the nondominant hand is facing down, again hooking your index fingers together briefly.

GIVE-UP/SURRENDER

Hold up both hands in fists in front of the body, palms facing outward, then pull both hands closer to the body while opening them into 5 handshapes.

TIP: Think of holding on to something tightly, then reluctantly releasing it.

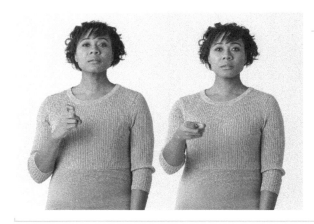

GIVE-YOU/GIVE-ME

Make an X handshape with your dominant hand and move the hand toward the person you are signing to. To sign GIVE-ME, move the hand toward your chest. This sign can also be done with a flat O handshape.

GLASS (CONTAINER) (See: Cup/Glass/Can, page 91)

GLASS (MATERIAL) (See: Tooth/Teeth/Glass [material], page 285)

GLOVES

With both hands in 5 handshapes, palms facing down, stack one hand on top of the other and pull the top hand closer to the body while keeping the fingertips in contact with the back of the opposite hand. Alternate the hands one time and repeat the movement.

TIP: Imagine pulling on gloves.

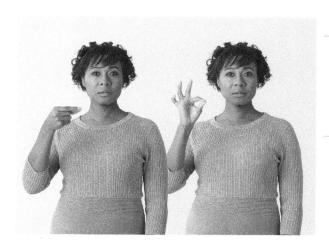

GLUTEN-FREE

Fingerspell the letters G-F with your dominant hand.

GO (See: Attend/Go, page 43)

GOAL

Make 1 handshapes with both hands. Hold your nondominant hand in front of your body, higher than your head. (It's important that your nondominant hand is higher up than your dominant hand.) Point your dominant index finger at your nondominant index finger and move toward it. They do not touch.

TIP: Imagine a desired future point that you are directing your thoughts to.

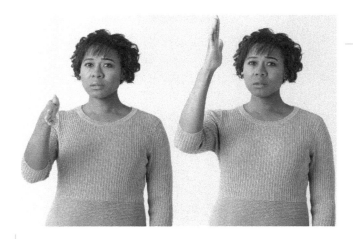

GOD

Make a flat B handshape with your dominant hand, palm facing to the side. Start with your hand positioned horizontally in front of your face on your dominant side. Bring the fingertips up in a semicircle, ending with your hand positioned vertically.

GODSON/GODDAUGHTER

This sign is a combination of GOD and SON (page 253). Your dominant hand first signs GOD in a flat B handshape, palm facing to the side. Start with your hand positioned horizontally in front of your face on your dominant side. Bring the fingertips up in a semicircle, ending with your hand positioned vertically. Then sign SON with both hands in flat B handshapes. Hold your nondominant hand up in front of your body, palm facing up, as if holding a baby. With your dominant hand, palm facing down, touch the side of your forehead (male reference), then bring the hand down on top of the nondominant arm, palm facing up. To sign GODDAUGHTER, combine the signs GOD and DAUGHTER (page 94): Make flat B handshapes with both hands. Position your nondominant hand in front of the body, palm facing up, as if holding a baby. With the fingers of your dominant hand, touch the side of the face near the chin (female reference point), then drop the hand down until it rests in the crook of your nondominant elbow with the palm facing up.

GOOD

With both hands in open handshapes, palms facing up, place the fingertips of your dominant hand on your chin. Bring the hand down to land on the palm of your nondominant hand.

TIP: Oftentimes, the nondominant hand is dropped in this sign. When this happens, the sign is the same as THANK-YOU (page 277). Context usually clarifies which meaning is intended.

GOOFY (See: Silly/Goofy/Ridiculous, page 245)

GRADUATE

Hold out your nondominant hand in an open handshape in front of your body, palm facing up. Position your dominant hand in a G handshape above your nondominant hand, tilting the hand forward while moving it down to land in your nondominant palm.

GRANDMA/GREAT-GRANDMA

Make a 5 handshape with your dominant hand, palm facing to the side. Touch your thumb to your chin, then move your hand forward, away from your face, in one or two arching movements.

Add another arching movement to communicate GREAT-GRANDMA.

GRANDPA/GREAT-GRANDPA

Make a 5 handshape with your dominant hand, palm facing to the side. Touch your thumb to your forehead, then move your hand forward, away from your face, in one or two arching movements.

Add another arching movement to communicate GREAT-GRANDPA.

GRASS

Make a claw handshape with your dominant hand, palm facing up, and touch the heel of your palm below your chin. Move the hand slightly forward, away from the chin, two times.

GREAT (See: Wonderful/Great, page 311)

GROUND (See: Area/Field/Ground, page 40)

GROW/PLANT (NOUN)

Hold out your nondominant hand in a relaxed handshape, palm facing inward. Make a flat O handshape with your dominant hand and position it below your nondominant hand. Move your dominant hand upward, between the thumb and index finger of your nondominant hand, while making a 5 handshape. If you repeat the movement two times, it becomes the sign for PLANT.

TIP: Think of a plant emerging from the ground and spreading its leaves as it grows bigger.

GROW-UP

Make a flat open handshape with your dominant hand, palm facing down. Start with your hand at waist height and raise it upward.

TIP: Think of your hand being on top of a child's head as they grow taller and taller.

GRUMPY (See: Angry/Grumpy/Mad, page 36)

GUESS/MISS

Make a 5 handshape in front of your face with your dominant hand, palm facing to the side, and move the hand across the face while closing it into a fist.

You can also use this sign to show MISS, as in "I missed the bus."

GYM (See: Exercise/Workout/Gym, page 116)

HAIR

Pinch and pull on your hair with your dominant hand.

HALLOWEEN

With both hands held in front of your face in flat open handshapes, palms facing inward, slide your hands from in front of your face to the sides of your head quickly two times.

TIP: It's like you're playing peek-a-boo.

HAMBURGER

Clasp both hands together, one on top of the other, then reverse the orientation so the other hand ends up on top.

TIP: Think of flattening a handful of ground beef into a patty.

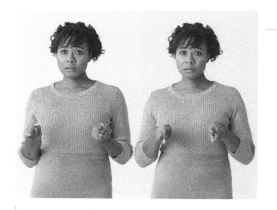

HAPPEN/WHEN (STATEMENT)

With both hands held horizontally in 1 handshapes, palms facing each other, twist your wrists to rotate the hands so that your palms are facing down.

You can also use this sign to communicate the word WHEN (used as a statement rather than a question).

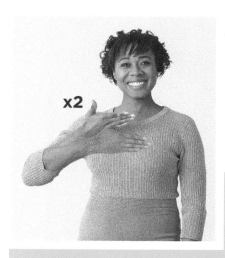

x2

HAPPY

Make a flat open handshape with your dominant hand, palm facing inward, and brush your hand up your chest in a circular motion two times.

TIP: A smile typically accompanies this sign, unless you want to show sarcasm, which would be communicated if you frowned while signing HAPPY.

HARD

With both hands in bent V handshapes, knock one fist down against the other one firmly.

TIP: You can emphasize the difficulty of something by making a strained facial expression.

HARD-OF-HEARING

Hold your dominant hand in front of your body in an H handshape, palm facing to the side, and tap the hand downward two times toward imaginary spots that are side by side.

TIP: HH is the abbreviation for hard of hearing.

HAT

Make a flat handshape with your dominant hand and tap the palm to the top of your head two times.

HAVE/DON'T-HAVE

With both hands in bent B handshapes, bring your fingertips to the sides of your chest, just inside the shoulder blades, in a firm movement.

TIP: If you shake your head side to side while making this sign, you are saying DON'T-HAVE.

HAVE-TO (See: Must/Need/Should/Have-To, page 200)

HAZARD (See: Danger/Hazard, page 93)

HE/SHE

Make a 1 handshape with your dominant hand and point toward the person you are referring to.

TIP: When referring to people who are not present, first communicate who you are talking about, then establish a reference point for them by pointing slightly downward at a spot in the space in front of you. Continue to refer to that same spot for any ongoing pronouns related to that non-present individual. Once the topic changes, new reference points can be established for new characters of reference. In ASL, pronouns are not gender specific.

HEALTHY (See: Brave/Confident/Healthy, page 62)

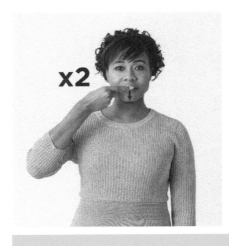

HEARING

Make a 1 handshape with your dominant hand, with the index finger held horizontally in front of the lips. Circle the finger away from the lips two times.

TIP: The finger circles out from your mouth as if words were spilling out of your mouth from talking.

HEART

Make a 5 handshape with your dominant hand, the middle finger extended forward and palm facing inward. Tap the middle finger to the heart area of your chest two times.

HELLO

Make a flat open handshape with your dominant hand. Touch the side of the index finger to the side of the forehead and bring your hand up and out as if saluting.

HELP

Hold out your nondominant hand in a flat open handshape. Make an A handshape with your dominant hand and rest it in the thumbs-up position on the palm of your nondominant hand. Raise both hands upward. Think of your bottom hand lifting up your top hand—providing support and help.

TIP: This is a directional sign, so you can move it forward to express HELP YOU, or move it toward you to say HELP ME. You can also show a Y/N? expression (page 7) while making this sign.

HERE

Point downward with the index fingers of both hands.

TIP: Think of pointing right at the spot where you are currently located.

HERS/HIS

Make a flat B handshape with your dominant hand and hold the palm at a 45-degree angle, then point the palm to the side. If you're talking about a specific person and they are near you, point the palm toward that person.

TIP: When referring to people who are not present, first communicate who you are talking about, then establish a reference point for them by pointing slightly downward at a spot in the space in front of you. Continue to refer to that same spot for any ongoing pronouns related to that non-present individual. Once the topic changes, new reference points can be established for new characters of reference. In ASL, pronouns are not gender specific.

HERSELF (See: Yourself/Himself/Herself, page 317)

HIGH-SCHOOL

Quickly fingerspell the letters H-S with your dominant hand.

HIKE/HIKING

With both hands in bent 3 handshapes, palms facing down or outward, move the hands forward alternately, mimicking feet taking steps.

HIMSELF (See: Yourself/Himself/Herself, page 317)

HIRE/INVITE/WELCOME

Hold out your dominant hand away from the body in a flat handshape, palm facing inward, and bring the hand in toward your torso.

The WELCOME concept of this sign refers to the greeting, not YOU'RE WELCOME.

HIS (See: Hers/His, page 156)

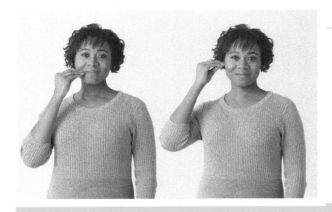

HOME

Make a flat O handshape with your dominant hand. Touch the fingertips to the side of your mouth, then move the hand up to the top of your jaw and touch the face again.

TIP: This sign indicates where you eat and where you sleep.

HONEYMOON

Make a 5 handshape with your dominant hand, the middle finger extended forward. Draw a short line down your chin with the tip of your middle finger on your dominant side, and then another on your nondominant side.

HONOR/RESPECT

With one or both hands in H handshapes near the forehead, one in front of the other, move them both forward, away from the head. This sign can be done with one hand or two.

TIP: People often bow their head down a bit while doing this sign. Think of tipping one's hat as a gesture of respect.

HOPE (See: Expect/Hope, page 117)

HORSE

Make an H handshape with your dominant hand. Touch the tip of your thumb to the side of your forehead and flap the two fingers up and down two times while keeping the fingers straight.

TIP: Think of the position of a horse's ear.

HOSPITAL

Make an H handshape with your dominant hand and draw a plus sign on the side of your nondominant arm.

TIP: Think the Red Cross.

HOT

Make a claw handshape positioned in front of your mouth with your dominant hand, palm facing inward, then quickly rotate the hand outward as you move it away from your mouth.

TIP: Think of putting something very hot in your mouth, then quickly spitting it out.

HOT-DOG/SAUSAGE

Make fists with both hands, palms facing down, and touch them together end to end. Open your fists slightly, moving your hands outward, then close them into fists again.

TIP: Think of connected sausage links that are pinched in sections to separate them.

HOTEL

Make a 1 handshape with your nondominant hand, palm facing to the side in a vertical position. Make an H handshape with your dominant hand, palm facing inward. Place the dominant hand on the tip of the nondominant index finger and tap the air toward your body with the dominant fingers.

HOUR/HALF-HOUR

Hold up your nondominant hand in a flat handshape, palm facing to the side. With your dominant hand in a 1 handshape, bring your palms together and make a clockwise circle with your dominant hand.

You can use a different number handshape (up to 9) to indicate 2 hours, 7 hours, etc. If you only make a half circle, you communicate HALF-HOUR.

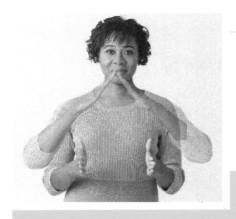

HOUSE

With both hands in flat open handshapes, palms facing each other and fingertips touching, move both hands apart and down in one motion.

TIP: The sign shows the roof and the walls of the house.

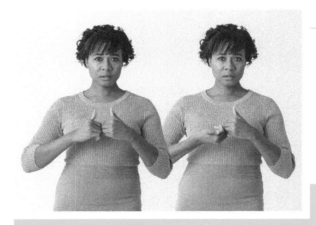

HOW

With both hands in bent B handshapes, knuckles together and palms facing inward, twist your dominant wrist to end with your palm facing up.

TIP: Show a WH? expression (page 7) while making this sign.

HOW-LONG (See: Long/How-Long, page 183)

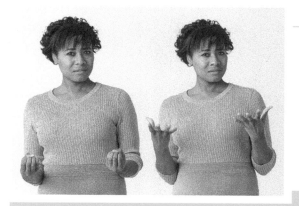

HOW-MANY/HOW-MUCH (MONEY)

With both hands in S handshapes in front of the body, palms facing up, open the hands upward into loose 5 handshapes.

TIP: Show a WH? expression (page 7) along with this sign. If you do this sign with one hand, you are asking how much something costs.

HOW-OLD (See: Age/Old/How-Old, page 29)

HUG (See: Love/Hug, page 185)

HUMID (See: Sticky/Humid, page 260)

HUNGRY

Make a C handshape with your dominant hand, palm facing inward. Touch your fingertips to the top of your chest and slide the hand downward, one time, to the stomach.

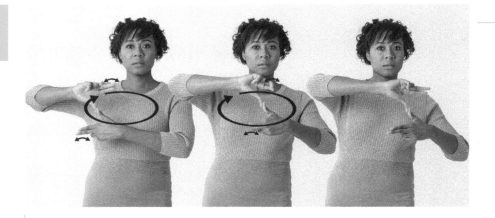

HURRICANE

Make H handshapes with both hands, the thumbs extended. The palm of your nondominant hand should face inward, and the palm of your dominant hand should face outward. Bring the tips of both thumbs together in front of your body, with the hands positioned horizontally. Bend your H fingers two times and move the hands in a circle while signing. You can also make this sign with flat hand-shapes instead of H handshapes.

HURT/PAIN

With both hands in 1 handshapes, point the index fingers at each other and twist the hands in the opposite directions.

TIP: This is a locational sign, so you can also make this sign in front of the area of the body that is hurting—for example, near the head to indicate a headache or near the mouth to indicate a toothache.

HUSBAND

Make relaxed C handshapes with both hands, the palm of your nondominant hand facing up and the palm of your dominant hand facing down. Touch the thumb of your dominant hand to the side of your forehead (male reference), then bring it down to clasp your nondominant hand, which is the sign for MARRIED (page 188).

I (See: Me/I, page 189)

I-LOVE-YOU

Hold up your dominant hand, palm facing outward, and extend your index finger, thumb, and pinky finger while the other two fingers remain folded down.

TIP: This is like signing the letters I, L, and Y all together on one hand. There are other ways to sign I-LOVE-YOU, but this one is the simplest. You can even wave the hand while it's in this handshape to say GOODBYE, I LOVE YOU.

ICE (See: Freeze/Freezer/Ice, page 134)

IDEA

Make an I handshape with your dominant hand and touch the fingertip of your pinky to the side of your forehead, then move the hand away from the body.

TIP: People often use an expression that communicates "I just thought of something!" when making this sign.

IF/SUPPOSE

Make an I handshape with your dominant hand and touch the fingertip of your pinky two times to the side of your head, near your eye.

TIP: This sign is typically done in a questioning way so make sure your face matches the type of question you are asking.

ILLNESS (See: Cold [illness], page 80)

IMAGINE (See: Visualize/Vision/Envision/Imagine, page 296)

IMPORTANT/VALUABLE

Make F handshapes with both hands in front of the body, fingers pointing forward and palms facing each other but not touching, then move the hands upward and curl them toward the center until your fists meet each other.

TIP: You can emphasize the value or importance of something by making a more intense expression and emphatic movement.

IMPROVE

Hold your nondominant arm in front of the body, palm facing down. With your dominant hand in a flat handshape, palm facing to the side, make a chopping motion near the wrist of your nondominant arm and then another chopping motion further up the same arm.

TIP: This sign can be modified in multiple ways to give further information. You can make multiple chopping motions close together as you move up the arm or just a couple of chops far apart to communicate a rate of improvement or the significance of growth leaps. You can also start the chopping motions up the arm and move them down to indicate a decline in progress.

IN/INSIDE

Hold out your nondominant hand in a relaxed O handshape. With your dominant hand in a flat O handshape, stuff the fingers one time into the opening made by your nondominant hand.

If you repeat the movement two times, it becomes INSIDE.

INFECTION/INSURANCE

Hold your dominant hand up near your shoulder in an I handshape, palm facing outward, and shake it side to side. People often scrunch up their face in disgust while doing this sign.

Without a facial expression, this sign is also INSURANCE.

INSENSITIVE (See: Sensitive/Insensitive, page 239)

INSPIRED

Hold both hands in flat O handshapes to the middle of your chest, palms facing inward. Move both hands upward while opening the hands into 5 handshapes.

INSTALL (See: Download/Upload/Install, page 106)

INSTRUCTIONS (See: Describe/Directions/Explain/Instructions, page 97)

INSURANCE (See: Infection/Insurance, page 168)

INTERESTING

With both hands in 5 handshapes, positioned in front of the chest, palms facing inward, pull both hands away from the body while shifting them into 8 handshapes.

TIP: This sign can also be done with L handshapes that start open and end with the two fingers pinched together.

INTERNET

With both hands in modified 5 handshapes, with the middle fingers extended forward, touch the fingertips of the middle fingers together in front of your body and twist your dominant hand slightly forward and back.

INTERNET-DOWN

Begin by signing INTERNET (page 169), then drop your dominant hand forward so that the fingers disconnect.

INTERPRET/ INTERPRETER

Hold up both hands in F handshapes and touch the pinched fingertips together. Twist one of the hands forward two times while maintaining contact.

If you add the PERSON sign (page 217) to the end of this sign, it becomes INTERPRETER. Sign PERSON with both hands in flat open handshapes, palms facing each other but several inches apart. Bring your hands straight down several inches while maintaining the handshapes and palm orientation.

INTERRUPT (See: Annoy/Bother/Interrupt, page 37)

INVENT (See: Create/Creative/Invent, page 90)

INVITE (See: Hire/Invite/Welcome, page 158)

ISLAM/ISLAMIC

Hold out your dominant hand in a modified C hand-shape, palm facing outward, and shake it.

JACKET (See: Coat/Jacket, page 79)

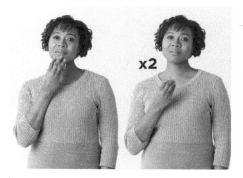

JEWISH/JUDAISM

Make a 4 handshape with your dominant hand, palm facing inward, and place the fingertips on the chin, with your thumb underneath your chin. Pull your hand down into a flat O handshape. Do this motion two times. It's important that your palm is facing your body and not to the side.

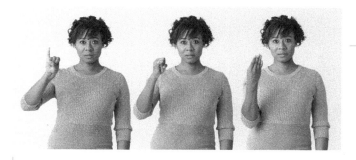

JOB

JOB is a lexicalized sign, meaning it involves fin-gerspelling in a specific way that has become a sign rather than just a string of letters. To sign JOB, first sign J with your dominant hand, and as you curve your hand in the J shape, quickly shift into the B hand-shape, with the palm turning inward.

JOIN/QUIT

Hold out your nondominant hand in a relaxed fist in front of the body. Make a U handshape with your dominant hand and push both fingers into the fist of your nondominant hand.

    If you start with the two fingers in the fist of the nondominant hand and then pull them out, this is the sign for QUIT.

JOKING/TEASING/KIDDING

With both hands stacked in X handshapes, your dominant hand on top, brush the top fist across the bottom fist.

TIP: Your facial expression while producing this sign can communicate whether the emotion behind it is silly or another feeling.

JUST (ADVERB) (See: Recently/Just [adverb], page 229)

JUST-ME

Make a 1 handshape with your dominant hand, palm facing outward. Twist your wrist downward and bring your hand to your chest, with your palm now in a vertical position facing inward.

KETCHUP

Hold up your nondominant fist, palm facing to the side. Make a flat handshape with your dominant hand and hit the top of your non-dominant fist with your palm two times.

TIP: Imagine hitting the bottom of a ketchup bottle to move the ketchup to the bottle opening.

KICK (See: Soccer/Kick, page 251)

KIDDING (See: Joking/Teasing/Kidding, page 172)

KISS-FIST (See: Love-It [kiss-fist], page 185)

KITCHEN

This sign is a combination of COOK (page 85) and ROOM (page 234). First, sign COOK by holding out your nondominant hand in a flat open handshape, palm facing up. With your dominant hand also in a flat handshape, clap each side of the hand down on your nondominant hand, as if cooking something on both sides. For ROOM, hold both hands horizontally in flat open handshapes, palms facing inward, and then bend both wrists back at the same time so that both palms face each other.

KNOCK-IT-OFF

Hold out your dominant hand in a 5 handshape, palm facing to the side, and shake the hand slightly a few times in the direction of the person you are talking to.

TIP: This sign is typically used to communicate a less firm request for someone to stop doing something. You could use either a joking or serious expression based on the emotion behind the request.

KNOW

Make a flat handshape with your dominant hand and tap your fingertips to the side of your forehead at the temple. You may often see this sign done by tapping the cheekbone for economy of motion. Both are correct forms of the sign.

If you reverse the orientation of this sign and push the hand outward after touching the face, it becomes DON'T-KNOW (page 103).

L

LANGUAGE

With both hands in F or L handshapes, palms facing to the side, touch the thumbs together, then move the hands out to the side, away from each other.

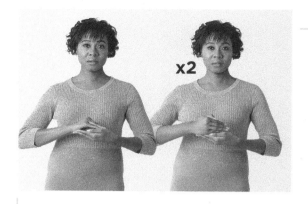

LAPTOP

Hold out your nondominant hand in a flat open handshape, palm facing up. Lay your dominant hand on top of your nondominant hand in the same handshape, palm facing down. Lift up the front side of your dominant hand while keeping the bottom portion of the hand connected to the other hand. Repeat two times.

TIP: Think of your hands representing a mini laptop and the movement of lifting the display screen open.

LARGE (See: Big/Large, page 54)

LAST/FINAL

With both hands in I handshapes in front of the body, palms facing inward, bring your dominant pinky down and lightly hit your nondominant pinky as it passes by.

TIP: Think of your pinky finger being the last finger on your hand.

LAST-WEEK/NEXT-WEEK

Hold the nondominant hand in front of your body, palm facing toward you or up. With the dominant hand in a 1 handshape, palm facing either forward or back, touch the wrist of the dominant hand to the wrist to the palm of the nondominant hand and move across the palm to the fingertips, then continue moving your hand back toward your shoulder.

If you move the dominant hand forward, instead of back toward your shoulder, it becomes the sign for NEXT-WEEK. Put a number on your hand (up to 9) to say how many weeks ago or how many weeks in the future.

LAST-YEAR (See: Next-Year/Last-Year, page 203)

LATE

Lift up the elbow of your dominant arm and let the hand dangle downward in a flat handshape with the palm facing inward. Swing your hand outward at the wrist twice, as if swatting at something.

LATER

Hold up your dominant hand in an L handshape near your head, palm facing outward, and drop the hand forward until your palm is facing down.

LAW/LAWYER

Hold up your nondominant hand in a flat open handshape, palm facing either up or to the side. Make an L handshape with your dominant hand, palm facing to the side, and tap your dominant palm on the upper portion of your nondominant palm. Move your dominant hand down, and then tap your dominant palm on the bottom portion of your nondominant palm.

You can add the sign for PERSON (page 217) after signing LAW to communicate LAWYER. Sign PERSON with both hands in flat open handshapes, palms facing each other but several inches apart. Bring your hands straight down several inches while maintaining the handshapes and palm orientation.

LAZY

Make an L handshape with your dominant hand and slap the palm on your opposite shoulder two times.

TIP: An uncaring facial expression typically accompanies this sign.

LEARN/STUDENT

Hold out your nondominant hand in a flat open handshape, palm facing up. Make a 5 handshape with your dominant hand and touch the fingers to the palm of your nondominant hand, then close your dominant fingers into a flat O handshape as you move the hand up to your forehead.

Add the PERSON sign (page 217) after LEARN to communicate STUDENT. Sign PERSON with both hands in flat open handshapes, palms facing each other but several inches apart. Bring your hands straight down several inches while maintaining the handshapes and palm orientation.

This sign is often shortened for economy of motion. Most people start by signing LEARN, but do not go all the way up to the head and instead just move the dominant hand down to the side, as if signing PERSON with just one hand.

LEAVE (DEPART)

With both hands in flat open handshapes in front of the body, palms facing down, pull both hands back toward your dominant shoulder, keeping the palms facing down while transitioning to A handshapes.

LEAVE (ABANDON)

With both hands in 5 handshapes, palms facing each other a few inches apart, drop both hands forward at the wrists as if you dropped something or left it behind.

LEFT (DIRECTION)

Hold out an L handshape with your dominant hand, then move it toward your left.

LESBIAN

Make an L handshape with your dominant hand and tap the index fingertip to your chin two times.

LET (See: Allow/Let, page 33)

LIBRARY

Make an L handshape in front of your body with your dominant hand, palm facing outward, and trace two small clockwise circles.

LICENSE (See: Certificate/Certified/License, page 72)

LIGHT

Make an 8 handshape with your dominant hand in front of your chin, palm facing inward, and flick your middle finger at your chin two times.

LIGHTNING

Make a 1 handshape with your dominant hand, palm facing outward, and draw a jagged downward line.

TIP: Think of drawing a lightning bolt in front of you.

LIKE

Make a 5 handshape against your chest with your dominant hand. Pull your hand outward, as if pulling a string, and as you pull, bring your thumb and middle fingers together in the middle.

LINK

With both hands in open handshapes, palms facing each other, bring the hands together as you shift into F hand-shapes and link your thumbs and index fingers together like links of a chain.

LION

Make a claw handshape with your dominant hand and position it above your head. Slide the hand across and down the back of your head, as if running your fingers through a thick mane of hair.

LITTLE/SMALL

With both hands in flat handshapes, palms facing each other a few inches apart, move your hands toward each other a couple of times. Pucker your lips as small as they will go when communicating that something is small in size.

TIP: This is a general sign to communicate that something is small in size, but there are many other ways to communicate smallness, relative to actual size.

LITTLE-BIT

Hold out your dominant hand, palm facing to the side, and flick your thumb off your index finger a couple of times.

TIP: While making this sign, squint your eyes as if trying to see a small amount of something.

LIVE/ALIVE

With both hands in A handshapes, position them near the bottom of your chest with the thumbs pointed up. Drag your hands up your body, ending near your shoulders.

LOAN (See: Borrow/Loan, page 58)

LONG/HOW-LONG

Hold up your nondominant arm, palm facing down. Make a 1 handshape with your dominant hand and draw a line with your index finger up the back of your nondominant arm, starting near your wrist and ending near your shoulder.

To ask HOW-LONG?, show a WH? expression (page 7) on your face while signing LONG.

LONG-TIME-AGO (See: Past/Long-Time-Ago, page 215)

LOOK-AT (See: See/Look-At, page 238)

LOOKS/LOOKS-LIKE/FACE

Make a 1 handshape with your dominant hand, palm facing inward, and trace a circle around your face with the tip of your finger. Don't touch your face—just circle the air in front of it.

If you add the sign for SAME (page 236) after this sign, you are saying LOOKS-LIKE.

LOSE (COMPETITIVE)

Hold out your nondominant hand in a flat hand-shape, palm facing up. With your dominant hand in a V handshape, smack your dominant palm in the center of the nondominant palm.

TIP: Think of a body doing a belly flop.

LOST (MISPLACED)

With both hands in flat O handshapes, bring your fingertips together in front of the body, and then twist both palms forward while opening the hands into 5 handshapes.

TIP: Think of holding something, then all of a sudden letting go of it.

LOUD/THUNDER

Make 1 handshapes with both hands, palms facing outward. Point both index fingers at your ears and pull them away, closing your hands into fists. Then shake the fists alternately from side to side near the head.

TIP: People usually make a startled expression with this sign, as though they heard a really loud noise.

LOUSY

Make a 3 handshape with your dominant hand, palm facing to the side, and touch the tip of your thumb to the tip of your nose. Move the hand forward, away from the nose, then drop it straight down.

TIP: Make a facial expression to match your level of dissatisfaction.

LOVE/HUG

With both hands in fists, cross your arms and touch the fists to the opposite shoulders, like a bear hug. If you hold the sign longer and shake the body a bit, you can indicate HUG.

LOVE-IT (KISS-FIST)

Make an S handshape with your dominant hand, palm facing outward. Place the back of the hand on your lips as if you are kissing it, then push the hand forward in a quick movement.

TIP: This sign for love is typically used to refer to non-affectionate, highly rated preferences such as "I love that new restaurant," "I love reading," or "I love the new teacher."

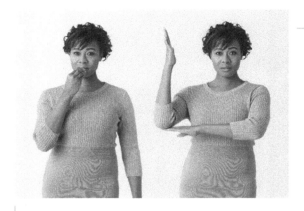

LUNCH

This sign is a combination of EAT (page 110) and NOON (page 205). First, sign EAT with a flat O hand-shape brought to your lips once, and then quickly sign NOON: Make flat handshapes with both hands and hold your nondominant arm horizontally in front of the body. Place your dominant elbow on top of the fingertips of your nondominant hand so that it is positioned vertically. Point the fingers of your dominant hand upward.

MAD (See: Angry/Grumpy/Mad, page 36)

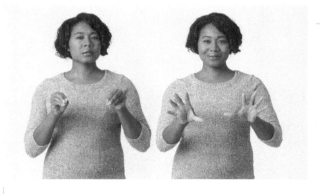

MAGIC/SPELL

With both hands in flat O handshapes, fingertips pointing away from the body, move the hands in half circles before opening both hands quickly into 5 handshapes.

TIP: Imagine sparkles flying out of your fingertips. A mysterious facial expression goes well with this sign.

MAKE/PRODUCE/MANUFACTURE

Make fists with both hands in front of the body and stack one on top of the other. Twist the fists in the opposite direction while maintaining contact.

TIP: Think of holding a strip of modeling clay and twisting it to make something out of it.

MAN

Make a 5 handshape with your dominant hand, palm facing to the side. Touch the thumb to your forehead (male reference point), then bring the hand down and touch the thumb to the center of your chest.

TIP: WOMAN (page 311) is communicated by making this same sign but while touching the lower part of the face (female reference point).

MANAGE/MANAGER (See: Control/Manage/Manager/Ruler, page 85)

MANNERS (See: Fancy/Formal/Manners/Polite, page 121)

MANUFACTURE (See: Make/Produce/Manufacture, page 187)

MARRIED/DIVORCED

Make C handshapes with both hands in front of your body, the dominant palm facing down and the nondominant palm facing up. Move both hands together until they clasp each other.

One way to sign DIVORCED is by signing MARRIED, then pulling the hands apart and to the sides after clasping them.

MATH

With both hands in M handshapes, palms facing each other, cross and uncross the fists two times, touching one to the other slightly as they pass each other.

MAYBE/MIGHT (VERB)

Hold out both hands in flat handshapes in front of your body, palms facing up. Move them alternately up and down two times.

TIP: Think of your hands as scales trying to weigh whether the answer will be a yes or a no.

ME/I

Make a 1 handshape with your dominant hand and point to your chest.

TIP: Indexing (page 9) is used in ASL to reference pronouns.

ME-TOO (See: Same/Me-Too, page 236)

MEAN (See: Rude/Mean, page 234)

MEANING/PURPOSE

Hold out your nondominant hand in a flat handshape, palm up in front of the body. With your dominant hand in a V handshape, touch the two fingertips to the center of your nondominant palm, then twist and touch the palm again.

MEAT

Hold out your nondominant hand in a flat hand-shape, palm facing to the side. With the thumb and index finger of your dominant hand, pinch the space between the thumb and index finger of your nondominant hand.

TIP: Think of holding up a slab of steak.

MEDICINE/MEDICAL

Hold out your nondominant hand in an open handshape, palm facing up. With your dominant hand in a 5 handshape, palm facing down, extend the middle finger and touch it to the center of your nondominant palm, then wiggle your dominant hand slightly.

MEDIUM/AVERAGE

With both hands in flat open handshapes, hold your nondominant hand up, palm facing inward. Make a chopping motion with the side of your dominant hand in the space between the thumb and index finger of your nondominant hand.

TIP: This sign is typically accompanied by a mouth shape that looks like you are making the M sound.

MEET-YOU

Make 1 handshapes with both hands, your nondominant hand facing inward and your dominant hand facing outward. The hands start apart from one another and come together with the knuckles of both hands touching.

TIP: Imagine that your index fingers are two people coming together face-to-face.

MEETING

Hold out both hands in relaxed 5 handshapes, palms facing each other and fingers pointed up. Bring all your fingers together as your handshapes change to flat O. Tap them together two times.

TIP: This sign communicates an official gathering of people, not just a casual meeting.

x2

MENSTRUATE

Make an A handshape with your dominant hand, palm facing inward. Tap your cheek with the fisted fingers two times.

MERCY (See: Pity/Mercy/Feel-Sorry-For, page 220)

MIDDLE-SCHOOL

This sign is a combination of CENTER (page 71) and SCHOOL (page 236). Hold out your nondominant hand in a flat handshape, palm facing up. With your dominant hand in a flat bent handshape, hover above the nondominant hand and make a partial circular movement before landing the fingertips in the center of the palm of the nondominant hand. For SCHOOL, with both hands in flat open handshapes, clap the palm of your dominant hand to the palm of your nondominant hand two times.

MIDNIGHT (See: Noon/Midnight, page 205)

MIGHT (VERB) (See: Maybe/Might [verb], page 188)

x2

MILK/DAIRY

Make a loose open S handshape with your dominant hand and squeeze it closed two times.

TIP: Think of the action of milking a cow.

MINE (See: My/Mine, page 200)

MINUTE

Hold up your nondominant hand in a 1 or flat handshape, palm facing to the side. Make a 1 handshape with your dominant hand and touch the fist to the center of your nondominant palm. Tick your index finger slightly forward.

TIP: You can incorporate a number into this sign (up to 9) to communicate 5 MINUTES, 8 MINUTES, etc.

MISCHIEVOUS/NAUGHTY

Make a 3 handshape with your dominant hand. Touch the thumb to the side of your forehead and bend the other two fingers a few times.

TIP: A sneaky expression goes well with this sign.

MISS (See: Guess/Miss, page 149)

MISS-YOU (See: Disappointed/Miss-You, page 100)

MISTAKE (See: Accident/Mistake, page 25)

MODIFY (See: Change/Modify/Adjust/Alter, page 73)

MOM

Make a 5 handshape with your dominant hand, palm facing to the side. Touch the tip of the thumb to your chin or tap it to your chin slightly two times.

MONEY

Make a flat B handshape with your nondominant hand and a flat O handshape with your dominant hand, both palms facing up. Tap the back of your dominant hand to the palm of your nondominant hand two times.

TIP: Think of slapping dollar bills against your palm.

MONKEY

With both hands in 5 handshapes, scratch your upper waist two times.

TIP: Think of a monkey scratching himself.

MONTH/MONTHLY/RENT (NOUN, VERB)

To sign MONTH, make 1 handshapes with both hands. Your nondominant hand is positioned vertically, palm facing outward, and your dominant hand is positioned horizontally, palm facing inward. In a downward motion, drag the dominant index finger down the back of the nondominant index finger one time. To sign MONTHLY or RENT, repeat the downward motion two or three times.

TIP: You can incorporate numbers into this sign (up to 9) by making a number with your dominant hand as you perform this sign. You can also communicate past or future (for example: 7 MONTHS AGO) by making a forward or backward movement with the dominant hand after the completion of the sign.

MOON

Make a bent L handshape with your dominant hand. Bend the index finger and touch the thumb to the side of your forehead, then lift the hand up higher and out to the side.

TIP: Most people do an upward glance toward their hand as they make this sign.

MORE

With both hands in flat O handshapes, touch all of the fingers together in front of the body two times.

MORNING

With both hands in flat open handshapes, hold up your nondominant arm in front of the body and touch the fingers to the crook of your dominant elbow. Lean the dominant arm forward with the palm facing up, then lift the arm toward you so that the palm rises to face you.

TIP: You can turn this into EVERY MORNING by sweeping this sign sideways toward the dominant side of the body.

MOSQUE (See: Temple/Mosque, page 276)

MOTHER-IN-LAW

This sign is a combination of MOM (page 194) and LAW (page 177). First sign MOM with your dominant hand in the 5 handshape, palm facing to the side. Touch the tip of the thumb to your chin or tap it to your chin slightly two times, and then smoothly transition to sign LAW. You sign LAW by holding your nondominant hand in a flat handshape with your palm facing to the side or upward. Your dominant hand is in the L handshape, palm facing the other hand. Tap the dominant hand to the palm of your other hand near the top, and then tap again at the bottom.

MOTORCYCLE/SNOWMOBILE

With both hands in fists and held out in front of the body as if holding handlebars, twist the wrist of your dominant hand back and forward two times as if revving a motorcycle.

For SNOWMOBILE, hold both hands up in the air near your head in 5 handshapes. Flutter your fingers as you move your hands down, then sign MOTORCYCLE.

MOUNTAIN/ROCK

With both hands in fists in front of the body, palms facing down, knock one fist down against the other, then lift both upward while opening the hands into 5 handshapes.

If you just do the knocking part of this sign two times and do not transition into the 5 handshapes, you are signing ROCK.

MOUSE (COMPUTER)

Make a claw handshape with your dominant hand, palm down and move it in small circles as if you were moving a cursor.

MOVE

Make flat O handshapes with both hands in front of the body, palms facing down. Raise your hands and move them to a different spot.

MOVIE/VIDEO

Make a flat open handshape with your non-dominant hand, palm facing inward, and make a 5 handshape with your dominant hand, palm facing outward. Place the dominant hand behind the nondominant hand and shake the dominant hand back and forth twice.

MUSIC/MUSICIAN/SONG

Hold up your nondominant arm, palm facing toward you. With your dominant hand in a flat handshape, thumb pointing upward, wave the hand side to side above your nondominant arm.

Add the PERSON sign (page 217) after the MUSIC sign to communicate MUSICIAN. Sign PERSON with both hands in flat open hand-shapes, palms facing each other but several inches apart. Bring your hands straight down several inches while maintaining the handshapes and palm orientation.

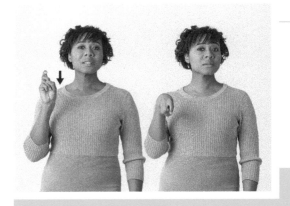

MUST/NEED/SHOULD/ HAVE-TO

Make an X handshape with your dominant hand, palm facing outward. Pull your hand downward.

TIP: The intensity of this sign and accompanying facial expression are very important to express the urgency of something. Should you clean your room, or do you have to clean your room?

MY/MINE

Make a flat handshape with your dominant hand and touch your palm to your chest.

MYSELF

Make an open A handshape with your dominant hand, palm facing to the side, and tap your chest two times with the back of your thumb.

NAME

With both hands in U handshapes, fingers pointing forward, tap the two fingers of your dominant hand against the two fingers of your nondominant hand two times.

NATURAL/NORMAL/REGULAR

Hold out your nondominant hand in a fist, palm facing down. With your dominant hand in an open N handshape, move the two outstretched fingers in a semicircle above your nondominant hand, then place them onto the back of the wrist.

NAUGHTY (See: Mischievous/Naughty, page 193)

NEAT

Pinch the thumb and index fingers of your dominant hand together and touch them to your cheek near your mouth. Twist your wrist forward once.

TIP: The location represents a dimple that shows in your cheek when you grin.

NEED (See: Must/Need/Should/Have-To, page 200)

NEPHEW/NIECE

Make an N handshape with your dominant hand. Twist the hand a couple of times next to the top side of the head (male reference).

The sign for NIECE is exactly the same but done on the lower part of the face (female reference).

NERVOUS

With both hands in 5 handshapes in front of your body, palms facing down, shake your hands as if you were very jittery.

TIP: When you sign NERVOUS, think of your hands shaking as though you had one too many cups of coffee.

NEVER

Make a B handshape in front of the face with your dominant hand, fingers pointing up and palm facing to the side, and move the hand as if drawing the number 7.

TIP: The intensity of your facial expression can communicate how committed you are to following through with your words.

NEW/FRESH

Make a flat open handshape with your nondominant hand and make an open bent handshape with your dominant hand. With your dominant hand, make a scooping motion on the palm of your nondominant hand, leading with the fingertips and going in the direction of the length of your nondominant hand.

NEXT-WEEK (See: Last-Week/Next-Week, page 176)

NEXT-YEAR/LAST-YEAR

With both hands in fists stacked in front of the body, dominant hand on top, flick out the dominant index finger while moving the hand forward or up. The nondominant hand remains in place.

LAST-YEAR is signed almost the same way, except the hand and flicking index finger face behind you, as if referring to the past. You can also incorporate numbers (up to 9) into this sign to show how many years in the past or future.

NICE (See: Clean/Nice, page 77)

NIECE (See: Nephew/Niece, page 202)

NIGHT/EVENING

Hold up your nondominant arm in front of the body, palm facing down. Make a bent B handshape with your dominant hand, palm facing down, and tap the wrist to the back of your nondominant hand.

NO

Make a relaxed 3 handshape with your dominant hand, palm facing outward, then pinch the three fingertips together quickly.

TIP: The intensity of this sign can communicate how firm you are in your response. Are you trying to say "nah"? If so, pinch the fingers together a couple of times without conviction.

NONE

With both hands in O handshapes, cross and then uncross the wrists quickly.

TIP: You can also just make the O handshapes and shake them slightly in front of the body.

NOON/MIDNIGHT

Make flat handshapes with both hands and hold your nondominant arm horizontally in front of the body. Place your dominant elbow on top of the fingertips of your nondominant hand so that it is positioned vertically. Point the fingers of your dominant hand upward.

To sign MIDNIGHT, do this sign the exact same way, except point the fingers of your dominant hand downward, below the arm.

NORMAL (See: Natural/Normal/Regular, page 201)

NORTH

Make an N handshape with your dominant hand, palm facing outward, and slide the hand straight up a few inches.

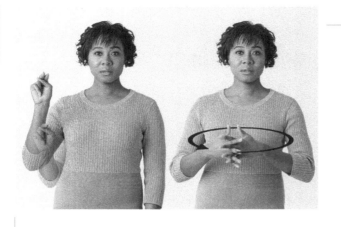

NORTH-AMERICA

This sign is a combination of NORTH (page 205) and AMERICA (page 35). Your dominant hand first signs NORTH with an N hand-shape, palm facing outward, by sliding the hand straight up a few inches. Then sign AMERICA with both hands in 5 handshapes, the fingers straight and interlaced and the palms facing inward. Move your interlaced hands in a counterclockwise circle.

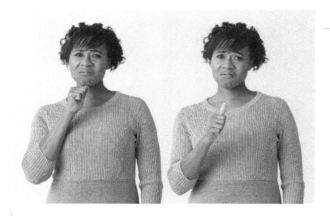

NOT/DON'T

Make an open A handshape with your dominant hand, palm facing to the side. Place the thumb under the chin and bring it forward, away from your body, in a swift movement.

TIP: Many of the negative signs push away from the body, as if distancing the signer from an unwanted object.

NOT-YET

Lift up the elbow of your dominant arm and let the hand dangle downward in a flat handshape with the palm facing inward. Swing your hand outward at the wrist twice, as if swatting at something. While doing this sign, open your mouth and stick your tongue out slightly.

TIP: While the mouth movement may feel silly, it is an important part of the sign. If you do not make the mouth movement, you will be signing LATE (page 176) rather than NOT-YET.

NOW/TODAY

With both hands in Y handshapes, palms facing up, pull both hands down quickly one time.

TIP: If you pull the hands down two times, it becomes the sign for TODAY.

NUMBER

With both hands in flat O handshapes, touch the fingertips together and twist them alternately in the opposite direction two times.

NURSE

Hold out your nondominant hand in a flat open handshape, palm facing up. Make a U handshape with your dominant hand and tap the two fingers to the wrist of your nondominant hand two times.

TIP: Think of taking someone's pulse.

NUTS

Make an A handshape with your dominant hand. Place the tip of your thumb under your two front teeth and pull the hand forward two times.

OBLIGATION (See: Responsible/Duty/Obligation/Chore, page 232)

OCEAN

Hold out both hands in 5 handshapes, palms facing down, and move the hands up and down like waves.

TIP: Some people sign WATER (page 300) before this sign.

ODD (See: Strange/Odd/Unusual, page 263)

OFFICE

With both hands in flat O hand-shapes, palms facing each other, flip the hands forward, one in front of the other, so that both palms face inward.

TIP: The motion of this sign is exactly like the sign for ROOM (page 234). There are several other ways to sign OFFICE. Defer to your local Deaf community.

OFTEN/FREQUENTLY

Hold out your nondominant hand in a flat handshape, palm facing up. With your dominant hand in a flat, slightly bent handshape, touch the tip of the fingers to the center of your nondominant palm, then touch further down toward your nondominant fingertips.

TIP: You can emphasize something happening very often by touching down more times and with greater speed and intensity.

OH-I-SEE

With your dominant hand in a Y handshape, palm facing outward, pump the hand forward a couple of times with an expression of comprehension.

TIP: This sign is excellent to show active listening while someone else is signing to you. When you do this sign, the other person knows you are engaged and following along.

OKAY (See: Fine [feeling]/Okay, page 127)

TIP: You can also fingerspell the letters O-K with your dominant hand.

OLD (See: Age/Old/How-Old, page 29)

ONCE (See: Twice/Once, page 290)

ONCE-IN-A-WHILE (See: Sometimes/Once-In-A-While, page 252)

ONION

Make an X handshape with your dominant hand and touch the index knuckle to the side of your face, next to your eye. Twist the hand forward two times while keeping the knuckle in contact with the face.

TIP: Think of how onions tend to make our eyes water when chopped or sliced.

ONLY/JUST

Hold up the index finger of your dominant hand, palm facing outward. Draw a small circle with the index finger as you twist the wrist so that the palm now faces toward you.

OPEN/CLOSED

With both hands in B handshapes, palms facing down and positioned side by side, shift the hands away from each other and turn the palms to face upward, as if opening a box.

To sign CLOSE, do this exact sign in reverse, ending with the hands positioned side by side and palms facing down.

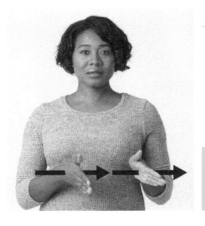

ORGANIZE/PLAN

With both hands in flat open handshapes, palms facing each other but several inches apart, slide both hands to the side.

TIP: Think of making neat rows of papers side by side on a desk in front of you.

OURS

Make a flat handshape with your dominant hand. Touch the side of the hand to your dominant shoulder, then circle the hand in front of the body in an arch, palm facing toward you, until the other side of the hand touches the other shoulder.

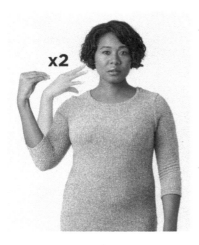

OUTSIDE

Hold up your dominant hand in a 5 handshape, palm facing inward, then pull the hand away from your body a couple of times as the fingers come together into a flat O handshape.

OWE (See: Bill/Debt/Due/Owe, page 54)

PAIN (See: Hurt/Pain, page 164)

PANCAKES (See: Cook/Pancakes, page 85)

PANTS

With both hands in flat handshapes, palms facing each other, slide them downward in front of each leg.

TIP: Imagine you are tracing the outline of each pant leg.

PARADE

Make 5 handshapes with both hands, palms facing down and fingertips extended toward the floor. Position your dominant hand in front of your nondominant hand and bend the wrists forward two times in quick movements.

TIP: Think of many legs walking together, as in a parade.

PARENTS

This sign is a combination of MOM (page 194) and DAD (page 92). With your dominant hand in the 5 handshape, sign MOM and then DAD in one smooth, quick motion, tapping the chin and then the forehead.

This sign is used for one parent or more than one parent, regardless of gender.

PARTNER

With both hands in bent 5 handshapes, palms facing inward, bring the hands together two times in front of your body, interlocking your fingers.

PARTY (See: Play/Party, page 221)

PASSOVER/CRACKERS

Make an A handshape with your dominant hand and knock the elbow of your nondominant arm with it two times.

The same sign is used for CRACKERS.

PASSWORD

This sign is a combination of PRIVATE (page 224) and WORD (page 312). For PRIVATE: With your dominant hand in an A handshape, touch the back of the thumb to the lips two times. For WORD: Make a 1 handshape with your nondominant hand, palm facing to the side. Make a G handshape with your dominant hand and touch the fingertips of the thumb and index finger to the top side of the nondominant index finger two times.

PAST/LONG-TIME-AGO

Make a flat open handshape with your dominant hand positioned above your dominant shoulder, palm facing behind you. Wave the hand backward a couple of times.

To show LONG-TIME-AGO, make bigger and more prolonged backward gestures with an emphatic facial expression.

PATIENCE/SUFFER

Make an A handshape with your dominant hand. Touch the back of the thumb to the front of your mouth and pull the hand downward past your chin.

TIP: A facial expression to communicate your level of patience or suffering goes well with this sign.

PAY/PAYMENTS

Hold out your nondominant hand in a flat handshape, palm facing up. With your dominant hand in a 1 handshape, touch the fingertip to the middle of your nondominant palm and sweep the finger forward past the fingertips.

You can show the plural concept of PAYMENTS by repeating this movement.

PAYCHECK

Start by making the sign for PAY by holding out your nondominant hand in a flat handshape, palm facing up. With your dominant hand in a 1 handshape, touch the tip of your index finger to the middle of the other palm and sweep the finger forward past the fingertips. Then make L handshapes with both hands, palms facing outward. Touch the sides of your index fingers and thumbs together, then move your hands apart, as if tracing the long edges of a check. Pinch each index finger and thumb together at the end to show the short edges of the check.

PEOPLE

With both hands in P handshapes in front of the body, palms facing down, move the hands alternately in circles.

PEPPER (SPICE)

Make an F handshape with your dominant hand and pantomime the sprinkling of pepper on a plate of food.

PERFECT

With both hands in F handshapes, palms facing each other but several inches apart, move the hands together until the pinched fingers of both hands come in contact with each other.

TIP: There are a lot of style and movement variations to this sign.

PERSON

Hold out both hands in flat open handshapes, palms facing each other but several inches apart. Move both hands straight down several inches while maintaining the handshapes and palm orientation.

TIP: Think of drawing the vertical position of an upright human.

PERSPECTIVE/VIEWPOINT

Hold out your nondominant hand in a 1 hand-shape, palm facing to the side. With your dominant hand in a V handshape, point the fingertips at your nondominant finger and rotate the position to look at the nondominant finger from another angle.

TIP: Think of getting two different viewpoints from one subject.

PET/SPOILED

Make a fist or a flat handshape with your non-dominant hand, palm facing down, then pet the back of that hand with your dominant hand in two quick strokes.

To communicate the verb of petting an animal or the concept SPOILED, draw out and slow down the petting strokes.

PHONE-CALL

This is a noun-verb pair. For PHONE, your dominant hand is in the Y handshape, held against your cheek. For CALL, bring your hand out a few inches away from your face.

PHOTO (See: Picture/Photo, page 219)

PICK (See: Find/Pick, page 126)

PICTURE/PHOTO

Hold out your nondominant hand in a flat hand-shape, palm facing outward (you can also do this sign with the palm facing sideways or inward). Make a C handshape with your dominant hand and touch the C hand next to your eye, then move it until it lands on your nondominant palm.

TIP: Think of seeing an image with your eyes, then putting it on a piece of paper.

PIE

Hold out your nondominant hand in a flat open handshape, palm facing up. Make a flat hand-shape with your dominant hand, palm facing to the side, and pantomime cutting a slice of pie on the palm of your nondominant hand.

PILL (See: Take-Pill/Pill, page 272)

PILLOW/CUSHION

With both hands in claw handshapes, palms facing each other but not touching, pulse your fingers a couple of times, as if squeezing something soft.

TIP: Make this sign by the cheek for PILLOW or in front of you for CUSHION.

PITY/MERCY/FEEL-SORRY-FOR

Hold out your dominant hand in a 5 handshape, palm facing down, and extend the middle finger slightly further than the others. Move the hand in a circular motion twice with a sympathetic facial expression.

TIP: You can also do this sign with two hands for emphasis.

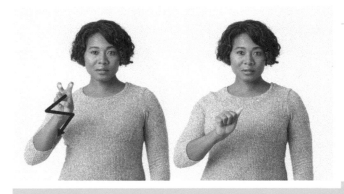

PIZZA

Make a bent V handshape with your dominant hand. Draw the letter Z with your hand, then close the fingers into an A handshape.

TIP: There are many other signs for pizza. Defer to your local Deaf community.

PLAN (See: Organize/Plan, page 212)

PLANT (NOUN) (See: Grow/Plant [noun], page 148)

PLATE (See: Dish/Plate, page 101)

PLAY/PARTY

With both hands in Y handshapes, arms held out horizontally in front of the body, move both hands side to side in tandem.

PLEASE

Make a flat open handshape with your dominant hand. Place the palm on your chest and move it in circles two times.

POLICE-OFFICER

Make a C (or modified C) handshape with your dominant hand and place the C over your heart, palm facing to the side. If you are left-handed, place the hand over the right side of your chest.

TIP: This sign resembles the badge on a police officer's uniform.

POLITE (See: Fancy/Formal/Manners/Polite, page 121)

POPCORN

Make fists with both hands, palms facing inward, and alternately flick the index fingers upward two or more times.

TIP: Think of popcorn as it pops up out of a hot pot.

POSSIBLE (See: Able/Possible, page 24)

POSTPONE/PROCRASTINATION

With both hands in F handshapes, palms facing each other, touch the pinched fingers together, then move your dominant hand forward while the other stays in place.

You can show PROCRASTINATION by repeating the movement and going further forward.

PRACTICE/REHEARSE/TRAIN

Hold out your nondominant hand in a 1 handshape, your finger pointing to the side and palm facing inward. With your dominant hand in an A handshape, palm facing down, brush the fisted fingers back and forth across the index finger of your nondominant hand.

TIP: You can show intensity through quicker and prolonged back-and-forth movements with a focused facial expression.

PRAY/WORSHIP

With both hands in flat open handshapes, press the palms together and move them in a slight inward circular motion.

TIP: This is very similar to the sign for ASK (page 42).

PREFER (See: Favorite/Prefer, page 123)

PRESSURE/STRESS

Make an S handshape with your non-dominant hand, palm facing to the side, and make a 5 handshape with your dominant hand. Rest your dominant hand on top of the S handshape. Push your nondominant hand downward two times with your dominant hand.

TIP: You're showing a bottle being pressurized again and again that will explode at any minute.

PRICE (See: Charge/Cost/Fee/Fine/Price/Tax, page 73)

PRIVATE/SECRET

Make an A handshape with your dominant hand and touch the back of the thumb to the lips two times.

PROBLEM

With both hands in bent V handshapes, palms facing inward, touch the backs of the knuckles to each other, then twist the wrists in the opposite directions and touch the knuckles together again.

PROCRASTINATION (See: Postpone/Procrastination, page 222)

PRODUCE (VERB) (See: Make/Produce/Manufacture, page 187)

PROGRAM (NOUN)

Make a flat open handshape with your nondominant hand, palm facing inward and fingers pointed up, and make a P handshape with your dominant hand. Place the P on the palm of your nondominant hand and slide it up, over, and down the backside of the hand.

PROMISE/COMMITMENT

Hold out your nondominant hand in an S handshape, palm facing to the side. Make a 1 handshape with your dominant hand, palm facing inward, touch your index finger to your lips, and then open the hand into a flat handshape and touch the palm to the top of your nondominant hand.

PROUD

Make an A handshape with your dominant hand, palm facing down, touch your thumb to your belly button area, and then pull it straight up to the top of your chest.

TIP: Think of zipping up a uniform that you are proud to wear.

PUNISH/DISCIPLINE

Hold your nondominant arm in front of your body, palm facing down. With your dominant index finger, reach over and touch the elbow of your nondominant arm by brushing past it.

PURPOSE (See: Meaning/Purpose, page 189)

QUEER (See: Rainbow/Queer, page 227)

QUESTION (See: Ask [question], page 42)

QUIT (See: Join/Quit, page 172)

RACE (See: Compete/Competitor/Athlete/Race, page 82)

RAIN

With both hands held up in 5 handshapes, palms facing outward, bend your wrists and lower your hands so your palms are facing down. Repeat this motion one more time.

RAINBOW/QUEER

Hold up both hands in 4 handshapes, palms facing inward, and move the dominant hand upward and back down as if drawing an arch.

TIP: Think of tracing a rainbow with your hand.

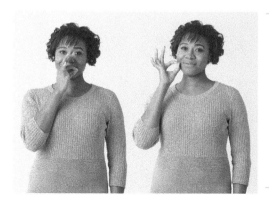

RAMADAN (FASTING)

Make an F handshape with your dominant hand. Place the pinched index finger and thumb on the corner of your mouth, on the nondominant side, and slide it across your lips to end at the opposite corner of your mouth.

RANCH/RANCHER (See: Farm/Farmer/Ranch/Rancher, page 122)

READ

Make a flat open handshape with your nondominant hand, palm up at a 45-degree angle, and make a V handshape with your dominant hand, palm facing down. Hold the fingertips of your V handshape in front of the nondominant palm and bend your wrist up and down.

TIP: Imagine that your bottom hand is a book. Your dominant hand is like eyes scrolling up and down the page.

READY

With both hands in R handshapes, palms facing outward, move both hands out to the side and back one or more times.

REAL-DEAL (See: Fact/Sure-Enough/Real-Deal/True-Biz, page 119)

REALLY/TRUE/SURE

Make a 1 handshape with your dominant hand, palm facing to the side, and touch the side of your index finger to your chin and mouth, moving the finger slightly upward and outward in an arch.

RECEIVE (See: Get/Receive/Acquire, page 140)

RECENTLY/JUST (ADVERB)

Make an X handshape with your dominant hand with the palm facing behind you. Place the side of your bent index finger next to your mouth. Open your mouth in a clenched-teeth expression when making this sign.

TIP: People often tilt their chin toward their dominant shoulder while doing this sign, especially to emphasize that something was very recent.

REFUSE

Make an A handshape with your dominant hand, thumb up and palm facing to the side, and move the hand over your shoulder with the thumb pointing behind you.

TIP: Use your facial expressions to emphasize firmness of refusal.

REGULAR (See: Natural/Normal/Regular, page 201)

REHEARSE (See: Practice/Rehearse/Train, page 223)

RELATIONSHIP

With both hands in F handshapes, link the fingers together as if they were links of a chain and bounce the hands forward and back two times.

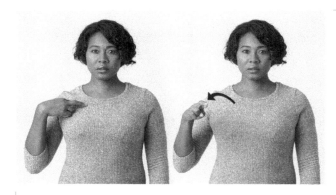

RELIGION

Make an R handshape with your dominant hand. Touch the tip of the fingers to your dominant shoulder, then rotate the palm forward as your hand moves away from the shoulder.

RELY-ON (See: Depend/Rely-On, page 97)

REMEMBER

With both hands in A handshapes, hold your nondominant hand in front of your body, thumb pointing up. Touch your dominant thumb to the side of your forehead, then bring it down to rest on the nondominant thumb.

RENT (NOUN, VERB) (See: Month/Monthly/Rent [noun, verb], page 195)

x3

RENTAL

Make 1 handshapes with both hands. Your nondominant hand is positioned vertically, palm facing outward. Your dominant hand is positioned horizontally, palm facing inward. In a downward movement, drag the dominant hand down the nondominant hand three times. This is the same sign as MONTH, but the repetition of the movement communicates RENTAL. Use this sign no matter the length of the time of the rental.

REPAIR (See: Fix/Repair, page 130)

REPEAT (See: Again/Repeat, page 29)

RESERVATION (See: Appointment/Reservation, page 39)

RESPECT (See: Honor/Respect, page 159)

RESPONSIBLE/DUTY/OBLIGATION/CHORE

With both hands in flat open handshapes, tap the fingertips to your dominant shoulder two times.

RESTROOM (See: Bathroom/Restroom/Toilet, page 48)

RIDE-IN/ON

Make a C handshape with your nondominant hand, palm facing to the side, and make a bent 2 handshape with your dominant hand, palm facing down. Hook the bent 2 fingers on the thumb of the C hand. Pull the C hand forward, moving the bent 2 hand with it.

TIP: Imagine a person sitting in a vehicle as it moves forward.

RIDICULOUS (See: Silly/Goofy/Ridiculous, page 245)

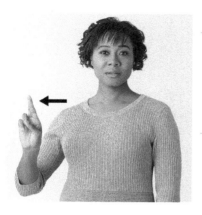

RIGHT (DIRECTION)

Make an R handshape with your dominant hand and move it toward your right.

RIGHT (CORRECT/ ACCURATE)

With both hands in 1 hand-shapes, palms facing to the sides in opposite directions and one palm positioned directly above the other, drop your dominant hand down on top of your nondominant hand.

RIGHT (LEGAL)

Hold out your nondominant hand in a flat hand-shape, palm facing up. With your dominant hand also in a flat handshape, touch the pinky side of the hand to your nondominant palm and slide it forward and upward.

ROCK (NOUN) (See: Mountain/Rock, page 198)

ROOM

With both hands held horizontally in flat open handshapes, palms facing inward, bend both wrists back at the same time so that both palms face each other.

TIP: Imagine making the four walls of a room.

RUDE/MEAN

Hold out your nondominant hand in a flat handshape, palm facing up. With your dominant hand also in a flat handshape, extend the middle finger forward to touch it to your nondominant palm and slide it from the heel of the hand past the fingertips.

If you make a claw handshape with the dominant hand and make the same movement, you can communicate MEAN (as in not nice).

RULER (See: Control/Manage/Manager/Ruler, page 85)

RUN

With both hands in L handshapes, index fingers pointing forward and one hand in front of the other, hook the index finger of the back hand around the thumb of the front hand and wiggle the front index finger as you move the hands forward.

RUN-AWAY (See: Escape/Run-Away, page 114)

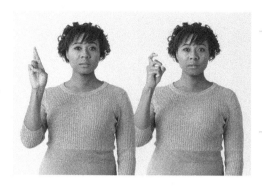

RX (PRESCRIPTION)

Sign the letters R-X quickly with your dominant hand.

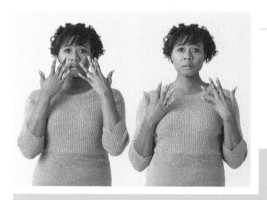

SAD

With both hands in front of the face in 5 handshapes, palms facing inward, pull both hands straight down several inches.

TIP: A sad expression accompanies this sign.

SALT

With both hands in V handshapes, rest one V on top of the other V and wiggle the two fingers of the top V handshape.

S

SAME/ME-TOO

Make a Y handshape with your dominant hand and slide it back and forth between the two things that are alike.

x2

SANDWICH

Make flat bent handshapes with both hands, palms facing toward the body or down, and stack one on top of the other in front of the mouth. Tap your fingertips to your mouth/chin area slightly two times.

TIP: Think of putting two slices of bread in your mouth.

SAUSAGE (See: Hot-Dog/Sausage, page 161)

SCARED (See: Afraid/Scared, page 28)

x2

SCHOOL

With both hands in flat open handshapes, clap the palm of your dominant hand with the palm of your nondominant hand two times.

SCIENCE/SCIENTIST

With both hands held up in A handshapes, palms facing outward, alternately trace circles with the hands as you move them in closer to the body.

Add the PERSON sign (page 217) after signing SCIENCE to express SCIENTIST. Sign PERSON with both hands in flat open hand-shapes, palms facing each other but several inches apart. Bring your hands straight down several inches while maintaining the handshapes and palm orientation.

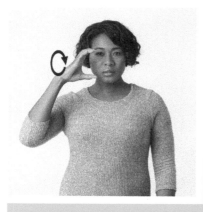

SEARCH

Make a C handshape in front of your face with your dominant hand, palm facing to the side, and move it in a circle.

TIP: Think of holding up a thick magni-fying glass to search for something. You can emphasize the intensity of the search through your facial expression. You can also use two hands rather than one.

SEASON

Make a flat open handshape with your nondominant hand, palm facing to the side, and make an S handshape with your dominant hand, palm facing outward. Place your dominant hand on the palm of your nondominant hand and circle your hand on the palm once.

SECRET (See: Private/Secret, page 224)

SEE/LOOK-AT

Make a V handshape with your dominant hand and point your fingertips at your eyes, then point them outward, or in a certain direction such as up at the sky or down at the ground, etc.

TIP: Think of your fingertips as eyes, and you can point them in the direction of what you are looking at.

SEE-YOU-LATER

Make an L handshape with your dominant hand and touch the thumb next to your eye on the same side of the body. Move the hand forward, away from the face as the hand arches downward.

TIP: This is almost the same as the sign for LATER (page 177), but it initiates next to the eye to indicate SEE.

SELL (See: Store [noun]/Sell, page 261)

SEND

Hold your nondominant hand in front of the body in a flat open handshape, palm facing down. Make a bent B handshape with your dominant hand and place the fingertips on the back of your nondominant hand. Flick the fingertips outward, ending with your dominant hand in the flat open handshape.

SEND-AN-EMAIL (See: Email/Send-An-Email, page 112)

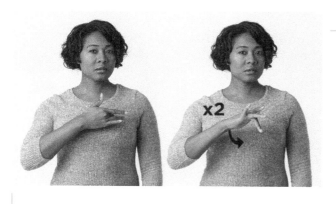

SENSITIVE/INSENSITIVE

Make a 5 handshape in front of your chest with your dominant hand, touch your middle finger to your heart area, and twist the wrist downward two times.

To communicate INSENSITIVE, add the sign for NOT (page 206): Make an open A handshape with your dominant hand, palm facing to the side. Place the thumb under the chin and bring it forward, away from your body, in a swift movement.

SERVE/SERVICER/SERVER

With both hands held out in flat handshapes, palms facing up, alternately slide the hands forward and back two or more times.

Add PERSON (page 217) to this sign to communicate SERVER or WAITER. Sign PERSON with both hands in flat open handshapes, palms facing each other but several inches apart. Bring your hands straight down several inches while maintaining the handshapes and palm orientation.

SHARE

With both hands in flat handshapes, hold the nondominant hand in place, palm facing inward, then swing the dominant hand back and forth between the thumb and index finger of your nondominant hand.

SHE (See: He/She, page 153, or You/He/She/I/Me, page 316)

SHEEP

Make a V handshape with your dominant hand and touch the back of the fingers in an upward circular motion to the top side of your nondominant arm.

TIP: Imagine that your nondominant arm is a sheep and you are using scissors to shear it.

SHIMMER (See: Sparkle/Shiny/Shimmer, page 255)

SHINY (See: Sparkle/Shiny/Shimmer, page 255)

SHIRT

Pinch and pull on your shirt with both hands, just inside the shoulder blades.

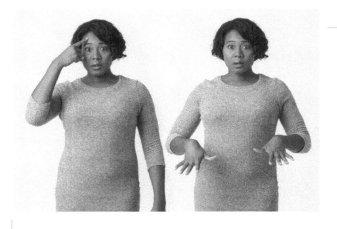

SHOCKED

Make a 1 handshape with your dominant hand, palm facing inward. Touch the index finger to the side of your forehead, then shift both hands into 5 or claw handshapes, fingers facing down, in a downward drop.

TIP: A shocked facial expression is an important nonmanual marker to accompany this sign. There are several other ways to sign SHOCKED. Defer to your local Deaf community.

SHOES

Hold out both hands in S handshapes, palms facing down, and knock the sides of the fists together two times.

SHOP/SHOPPING (See: Buy/Shop/Shopping, page 67)

SHORTS

Make flat bent handshapes with both hands and make a chopping motion against your upper thighs.

SHOULD (See: Must/Need/Should/Have-To, page 200)

SHOW (VERB)

Hold out your nondominant hand in a 5 handshape, palm facing to the side or outward. Make a 1 handshape with your dominant hand and touch the center of your nondominant palm with your index finger, then move both hands forward.

TIP: Imagine pointing at a picture you drew and showing it to someone. This sign is also directional, so if you move your hands toward you, rather than away from you, you are saying SHOW ME.

SHOWER

Make a fist to the side and above your head with your dominant hand. Open your hand into the 5 handshape two times.

TIP: Think of water coming out of the showerhead.

SHY

Hold up your dominant hand in a loose A handshape, palm facing down, and touch your knuckles to your cheek, then rotate the hand against your cheek so that the palm faces behind you.

SICK

With both hands in 5 handshapes, the middle fingers extended forward, place the tip of your dominant middle finger on the side of your forehead and the tip of your nondominant middle finger on the side of your stomach.

TIP: Show an expression of not feeling well with this sign.

SIGN (VERB)

With both hands in fists, palms facing to the side, open them into 5 handshapes and then close them back into fists one or more times.

TIP: You can also move the hands alternately in forward circles as you open and close your fists.

SIGN-LANGUAGE (NOUN)

With both hands in 1 handshapes, palms facing each other, hold up the index fingers and move them in alternating circular motions toward the body.

SILLY/GOOFY/RIDICULOUS

Hold a Y handshape in front of your nose, palm facing to the side, and twist your wrist back and forth.

To sign RIDICULOUS, make only one large movement with the Y handshape rather than a repeated movement.

SINCE (See: Up-Until-Now/Since, page 292)

SINGLE

Make a 1 handshape with your dominant hand. Touch the side of the index finger to the side of your mouth, then pull the finger downward. Repeat the same movement on the other side of the mouth.

SISTER

Hold your nondominant hand in front of the body in an L handshape, palm facing inward. Make an A or L handshape with your dominant hand and place the thumb on the cheek, near the mouth (female reference). Bring your dominant hand down on top of your nondominant hand, shifting into an L handshape as it lands.

SIT (See: Chair/Sit, page 72)

SKILL/TALENT

Hold up your nondominant hand in a flat handshape, palm facing to the side. Make a flat handshape with your dominant hand as well. Grab the bottom side of your nondominant hand and pull your dominant hand downward into an A handshape.

SKIN

Using your thumb and your bent index finger, pinch your cheek.

SKIRT

With both hands in 5 handshapes, palms facing down, touch the heels of your hands to your hips and then slide them downward.

SKY

Make a B handshape with your dominant hand and move it in a sweeping sideways gesture over your head, as if referencing the sky.

SLEEP/SLEEPY

Hold up your dominant hand in front of your face in a 5 handshape and close the fingers into a flat O handshape as your hand moves downward. If you repeat the movement gently a couple of times with a tired facial expression, you can communicate SLEEPY.

TIP: Think of your eyes closing.

SLOW/SLOWLY

With both hands in 5 handshapes, palms facing down, place your dominant hand on top of your nondominant hand. Drag the dominant hand up until your fingertips are near the wrist of your nondominant hand.

TIP: This motion is done somewhat slowly. To demonstrate the degree of slowness, you can slow down the movement.

SMALL (See: Little/Small, page 181)

SMART

Make a 5 handshape with your dominant hand, palm facing to the side. Touch the tip of your middle finger to the side of your forehead, then rotate the palm to face outward.

SMOKE/FOG

With both hands in claw handshapes, one palm facing up and one palm facing down, move the hands in opposite circles while keeping the palms facing each other.

    If you do this near your face with a facial expression that indicates a struggle to see clearly, you can communicate FOG.

SNAKE

Make a bent V handshape with your dominant hand, palm facing outward. Touch the knuckles to your chin and move the hand forward in a squiggly line.

TIP: Think of your bent fingers as the fangs of a snake and the squiggly line as a slithering motion.

SNEEZE

Make a 1 handshape with your dominant hand, palm facing down, and touch the side of the index finger to the space under your nose while dropping your head forward forcefully.

TIP: Think of the body movement that often accompanies a powerful sneeze.

SNOW

Hold both hands in the air near your head in 5 handshapes. Flutter your fingers as you move your hands down.

TIP: If it is softly falling snow, you can rock the hands slightly from side to side as they move down.

SNOWMOBILE (See: Motorcycle/Snowmobile, page 197)

SOCCER/KICK

Hold out your nondominant hand in a flat open handshape, palm facing to the side or inward. Make a B handshape with your dominant hand, palm facing to the side, and knock it against the bottom of your nondominant hand two times.

Make just one emphasized knocking movement to communicate KICK.

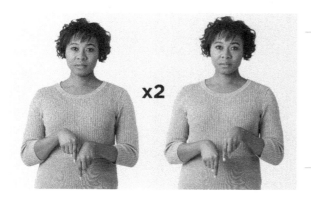

SOCKS

With both hands in 1 handshapes, index fingers pointing down, rub both fingers up and down against each other twice.

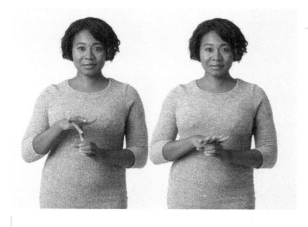

SODA

Hold out your nondominant hand in a fist, palm facing to the side. With your dominant hand in a 5 handshape, touch the middle finger to the top of your nondominant fist, then immediately touch the entire palm to the fist.

SOMEDAY (See: Future/Someday, page 139)

SOMETHING/SOMEONE

Make a 1 handshape with your dominant hand, palm facing inward and index finger pointing up. Wiggle the hand very slightly side to side.

TIP: If you make a bigger side-to-side movement, you are signing ALONE (page 34).

SOMETIMES/ONCE-IN-A-WHILE

Hold out your nondominant hand in a flat handshape, palm facing up or to the side. Make a 1 handshape with your dominant hand and touch the side of your index fingertip to your nondominant palm in a circular motion a couple of times.

To communicate something happening only ONCE-IN-A-WHILE, make a bigger circular motion.

SON

Make flat B handshapes with both hands. Hold your nondominant hand up in front of your body, palm facing up, as if holding a baby. With your dominant hand, palm facing down, touch the side of your forehead (male reference), then bring the hand down on top of the nondominant arm, palm facing up.

SONG (See: Music/Musician/Song, page 199)

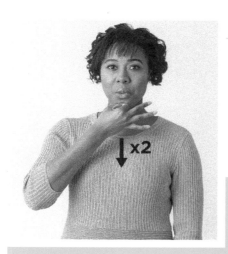

SOON

Make an F handshape with your dominant hand, palm facing inward and held horizontally. Place the pinched fingers on your chin and move them downward a couple of times.

TIP: Your mouth is in a pursed O shape, as if you were blowing out candles on a cake.

SORRY

Make an S or A handshape with your dominant hand. Place it on your chest and move it in a circle a couple of times.

SOUTH

Make an S handshape with your dominant hand, palm facing outward, and slide the hand straight down a few inches.

SOUTH-AMERICA

This sign is a combination of SOUTH and AMERICA (page 35). Your dominant hand first signs SOUTH with an S handshape, palm facing outward, by sliding the hand straight down a few inches. Then sign AMERICA with both hands in 5 handshapes, the fingers straight and interlaced and the palms facing inward. Move your interlaced hands in a counterclockwise circle.

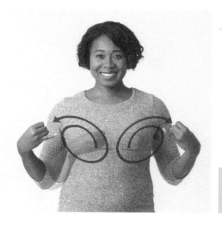

SPAGHETTI

Make I handshapes with both hands, palms facing inward, and point the pinkies toward each other. Move the pinkies away from each other while making curling motions.

TIP: Think of curly spaghetti noodles.

SPARKLE/SHINY/SHIMMER

Hold up your nondominant hand in a fist or flat handshape, palm facing down. Make a 5 handshape with your dominant hand and touch the middle finger to the back of the nondominant hand, then pull away while twisting the hand repeatedly as it moves back.

TIP: This sign can originate from multiple places, depending on what is being described. For example: a radiant diamond ring, sparkling eyes, twinkling stars, etc.

SPECIAL

Hold up the index finger of your nondominant hand, palm facing to the side or inward, and pinch it together with the index finger and thumb of your dominant hand while pulling upward.

TIP: Think of your nondominant index finger as being the chosen one.

SPELL (See: Magic/Spell, page 186)

SPELL (See: Magic/Spell, page 186)

SPILL-CUP

Make a C handshape with your dominant hand and tip your hand forward, as if you were spilling your cup.

SPOILED (See: Pet/Spoiled, page 218)

SPOILED (See: Pet/Spoiled, page 218)

SPOON/SOUP

Make a slightly curved H handshape with your dominant hand and move the hand in a circular, clockwise motion in front of the mouth.

If you hold out a cupped handshape with your nondominant hand, palm facing up, while making the sign for SPOON, it becomes the sign for SOUP.

SPRING

Make a flat C handshape with your nondominant hand, palm facing inward, and make a flat O handshape with your dominant hand, palm facing inward as well. Place the fingertips of the dominant hand in the space inside the flat C hand. Push your dominant hand up through the opening, and as you do, open the hand into a 5 handshape. Repeat this motion two times.

ST.-PATRICK'S-DAY

Pinch your dominant thumb and index finger together and touch them to the bicep of your nondominant arm. Twist the hand once, as if pinching and twisting the skin. Follow with the sign for DAY (page 94): Hold your nondominant arm in front of your body, palm facing inward or down. Make a 1 handshape with your dominant hand and rest the elbow on top of the fingers of your nondominant hand with your index finger pointing straight up. Drop your dominant arm down to the side to land on top of your nondominant arm.

STAND

Hold out your nondominant hand in a flat hand-shape, palm facing up. With your dominant hand in a V handshape, touch the two fingertips to the center of the nondominant palm, like legs standing on a flat surface.

TIP: If you move the hands in a forward circular movement while making this sign, you are communicating standing for a long period of time.

STAR

With both hands in 1 handshapes, hold them side by side next to or above your head. Alternately rub your two fingers up and down against each other twice.

TIP: People usually look up at their hands while doing this sign, as if they are gazing at stars in the sky.

START

Make a 5 handshape with your nondominant hand and make a 1 handshape with your dominant hand. Place the index finger of your dominant hand in the webbing between the index and middle finger of your nondominant hand. Twist your finger outward once, as if you were starting your car—your finger represents your keys.

STATE (NOUN)

Hold up your nondominant hand in a flat open handshape with the palm facing away from the body. Make an S handshape with your dominant hand and knock the side of the fist at the top of your nondominant hand and again at the bottom.

STEAL

Hold out your nondominant arm, palm facing down. With your dominant hand in a V handshape, touch the fingers to the elbow of your nondominant arm and pull the hand back while bending the fingers into a bent V handshape.

TIP: You can repeat this movement to show a repeated pattern of theft.

STEP

Hold out your dominant hand in an L handshape, the finger pointing away from the body and the palm facing to the side. Tilt the wrist sideways so that your palm now faces up.

TIP: Combine this with a family member sign to communicate STEP-DAD (for DAD, see page 92), STEP-SISTER (for SISTER, see page 246), etc.

STICKY/HUMID

With both hands in 5 handshapes, palms facing up, pinch the thumbs and middle fingers together while moving the hands up and down two or more times.

TIP: You can also do this sign with just one hand.

STILL/STAY

With both hands in Y handshapes, palms facing inward or down, hold them close to the body at first, then slide them both forward simultaneously.

For STAY, you just move both hands slightly downward one time rather than sliding them forward.

STOP

Hold out your nondominant hand in a flat handshape, palm facing up. With your dominant hand also in a flat handshape, make a chopping motion one time on your nondominant palm.

x2

STORE (NOUN)/SELL

With both hands in flat O handshapes in front of the body, palms facing down, flick your wrists up two times.

To communicate SELL, make one forward movement instead of two.

STORE (VERB)/SAVE

Hold out your nondominant hand in a fist, palm facing to the side. Make a V handshape with your dominant hand and tap the two fingers on the bottom of your nondominant fist two times.

STORM (See: Clouds/Storm, page 79)

STORY

Pinch all of the fingers from both hands together, then pull the hands apart and shift the wrists in opposite directions while opening the fingers, then, pinching the fingers together again.

TIP: You can exaggerate this sign to indicate a long or in-depth story.

STRAIGHT/HETEROSEXUAL/SOBER

Make a B handshape with your dominant hand, palm facing to the side, and touch the index finger to your nose. Move the hand forward, away from your face, in a straight line.

STRANGE/ODD/UNUSUAL

Make a C handshape with your dominant hand in front of your face, palm facing to the side. Drop the hand down from the wrist so that the palm then faces down.

A suspicious facial expression goes well with this sign.

STREAMING

Make 4 handshapes with one or both hands and position them above your dominant shoulder, one higher than the other, with the fingers pointing forward. Move the hands up and down two times.

TIP: Think of pulling down information from "the cloud."

STRESS (See: Pressure/Stress, page 224)

STRICT

Make a bent V handshape with your dominant hand and touch the side of the index finger knuckle to your nose.

TIP: You can emphasize strictness by using all four bent fingers rather than just two.

STROKE (MEDICAL)

Make a flat open handshape with your dominant hand, palm facing to the side. Starting at the forehead, draw a zigzagging line in the space in front of the body.

TIP: There are other ways to sign this word. Always defer to your local Deaf community.

STRONG

Make fists with both hands, palms facing inward, near the dominant shoulder. Pull both fists forward forcefully, away from the body, in the same direction.

STRUGGLE

Make 1 handshapes with both hands and hold up both index fingers, pointing them directly at each other. Move the hands in circular motions at the same time, keeping the fingers pointing at each other.

STUBBORN

Hold up the dominant hand in a flat handshape, palm facing outward, with the thumb touching the side of your forehead. Fold the other fingers down so that the hand is now in an A handshape.

STUCK/TRAPPED/CLOGGED

Make a V handshape with your dominant hand and poke both fingertips directly in the middle of your neck.

STUDENT (See: Learn/Student, page 178)

STUDY

Hold out your nondominant hand in a flat hand-shape, palm facing up. With your dominant hand in a 5 handshape, point and wiggle your fingertips in the direction of the nondominant palm.

SUBWAY

Make a B handshape with your nondominant hand, palm facing down, and make a Y handshape with your dominant hand, palm facing outward. Place your dominant hand underneath your nondominant hand. Move your dominant hand forward and backward two times.

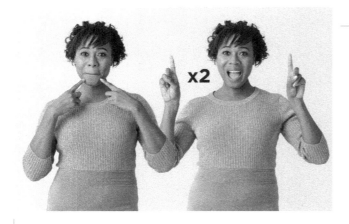

SUCCESS/FAMOUS

With both hands in 1 hand-shapes, palms facing inward, place the tips of your index fingers on the sides of your chin. Twist your palms outward and inward two times while moving your hands up higher.

SUFFER (See: Patience/Suffer, page 215)

SUMMER

Make a 1 handshape with your dominant hand held in front of your forehead, palm facing down. Drag your finger to the other side of your forehead and shift your hand into an X handshape as you move it.

SUN/SUNSHINE/SUNLIGHT

Make a C handshape with your dominant hand, palm facing to the side, and tap the side of the hand to the side of your forehead, next to your eye.

TIP: You can also make this sign by moving the C handshape up toward the sky.

SUNRISE/SUNSET

Hold out your nondominant arm, palm facing down. Make a C or F handshape with your dominant hand and position it below the opposite elbow, then move it upward the way a sun would rise above a horizon.

To sign SUNSET, make the same sign but position the moving hand above the elbow and drop it down, like a setting sun.

SUPPER (See: Dinner/Supper, page 99)

SUPPORT

Make S handshapes with both hands, palms facing inward. Hold your nondominant hand horizontally while the dominant hand comes up from underneath and lifts the nondominant fist up a few inches.

TIP: To communicate this as a verb, make two lifting movements with the fist rather than one.

SUPPOSE (See: If/Suppose, page 166)

SURE (See: Really/True/Sure, page 229)

SURE-ENOUGH (See: Fact/Sure-Enough/Real-Deal/True-Biz, page 119)

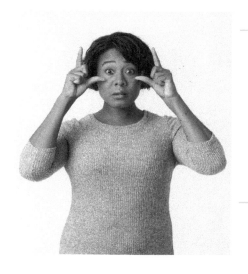

SURPRISE/WAKE-UP

With both hands in fists, extend the index fingers and thumbs and pinch them together next to the eyes. Open your eyes suddenly with an expression of surprise.

WAKE-UP is signed the same way, but usually with a groggy expression.

SURRENDER (See: Give-Up/Surrender, page 142)

SWEET/SWEETIE

Make a flat open handshape with your dominant hand, palm facing inward. Place your fingertips on the tip of your chin and bend your fingers so they slide down and off the chin. The movement can be repeated.

SWEETHEART

With both hands in A handshapes, palms facing inward, bring the knuckles of both hands together in front of the heart and wiggle both thumbs up and down from the top knuckles.

TIP: In English we often use this word as a term of endearment in relationships that are either romantic or nonromantic. This ASL sign, however, implies a romantic connection. If you want to communicate sweetheart in reference to a child or nonromantic partner, you could use the sign for SWEET/SWEETIE (page 269).

SWIM

This is basically a pantomime. Make swim strokes in whatever way you choose.

SYSTEM

With both hands in Y handshapes, palms facing down or outward and the thumbs touching, move your hands apart a few inches and then straight down.

TABLE

Make flat handshapes with both hands, palms facing down. Bring your arms up in front of your body, parallel to the ground, positioning your dominant arm above your nondominant arm, and clap the top arm down on the bottom arm two times.

TAKE-CARE-OF (See: Careful/Take-Care-Of, page 70)

TAKE-PILL/ PILL

Make a fist with your dominant hand, extend the thumb and index fingers, and press the fingernail of your index finger to the tip of the thumb. Bring your hand toward your mouth and flick your index finger in the direction of your slightly open mouth, as if popping a pill. If you flick the finger two times, it becomes PILL (noun).

TALENT (See: Skill/Talent, page 247)

TALK (See: Chat/Talk, page 73)

TATER-TOTS (See: French-Fries/Tater-Tots, page 135)

TAX (See: Charge/Cost/Fee/Fine/Price/Tax, page 73)

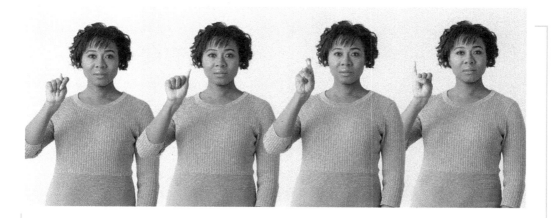

TAXI

Fingerspell the letters T-A-X-I with your dominant hand.

TEA

Hold out your nondominant hand in a C handshape or fist with the palm facing inward, as if holding a mug. Make an F handshape with your dominant hand and move it in circles above the opposite fist, as if swirling a tea bag around in a teacup.

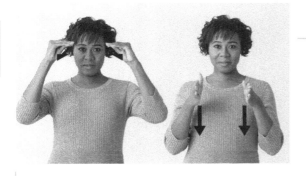

TEACH/TEACHER

With both hands in flat O hand-shapes held in front of your forehead, palms facing each other, move the hands away from the head, then immediately sign PERSON (page 217): With both hands in flat open handshapes and the palms facing each other a few inches apart, bring your hands straight down.

TIP: Think of the sign for TEACH as representing someone taking knowledge out of their minds and giving it to someone else.

TEAM

With both hands in T handshapes in front of your body, the thumbs touching and palms facing outward, move the hands out to the side and arch them forward until the hands meet again on the pinky side with the palms facing inward.

TIP: This is the same motion as FAMILY (page 120) and DEPARTMENT (page 96), with a different letter handshape.

TEASING (See: Joking/Teasing/Kidding, page 172)

TECHNOLOGY

Make a flat open handshape with your non-dominant hand, palm facing to the side and held vertically. Make a 5 handshape with your dominant hand, the middle finger extended forward. With the tip of your dominant middle finger, tap the bottom side of your nondominant hand two times.

TEMPERATURE

Hold up your nondominant hand in a 1 hand-shape, palm facing outward. Make a 1 handshape with your dominant hand as well, palm facing inward, and slide the index finger up and down the back of the nondominant index finger.

TIP: Think of how mercury rises or falls in a thermometer.

TEMPLE/MOSQUE

Make an S handshape with your nondominant hand, palm facing down, and make a T handshape with your dominant hand, palm facing outward. Tap the base of your dominant hand on the back of your nondominant hand two times.

For MOSQUE, complete the same sign with the dominant hand in an M handshape.

TENDS-TO/TYPICALLY

With both hands in 5 handshapes in front of your chest, palms facing inward, extend the middle fingers of both hands forward to touch the chest, then pull both hands away from the body at the same time while keeping the palms facing inward.

TERRIBLE (See: Awful/Terrible, page 45)

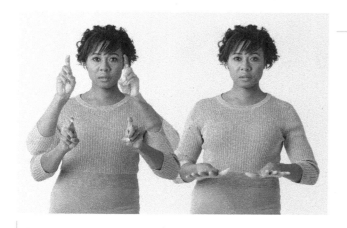

TEST/EXAM

With both hands held up in X handshapes, palms facing outward, flex your index fingers up and down as you move the hands downward, then change your hands into 5 handshapes, palms facing down, toward the end of the movement.

THANK-YOU/ YOU'RE-WELCOME

Make a flat open handshape with your dominant hand, palm facing inward. Touch your fingertips to your mouth/chin area and move your hand forward without reversing the palm.

TIP: If someone signs THANK-YOU to you, you simply sign THANK-YOU right back at them to communicate YOU'RE-WELCOME.

THANKSGIVING

With both hands in flat open handshapes, palms facing inward, place the finger-tips of both hands on or near your chin and move both hands outward, away from your body, at the same time.

TIP: You are basically signing THANK-YOU (page 277) but with both hands instead of one.

THEMSELVES

Make an A handshape with your dominant hand, the thumb pointing upward and palm facing to the side. Push the fist forward two times in the direction of whoever you are referring to. If you are referring to more than one person, sweep the hand sideways while making this sign.

TIP: Refer to the signing Tip for YOU (page 316) for instructions on how to refer to individuals who are not physically present. Pronouns in ASL are not gender specific.

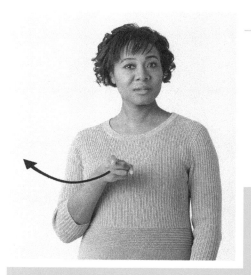

THEY/THEM

Use the index finger of your dominant hand to point at the person you are referring to. If you are referring to more than one person, then sweep the hand sideways while pointing.

TIP: Refer to the signing Tip for YOU (page 316) for instructions on how to refer to individuals who are not physically present. Pronouns in ASL are not gender specific.

THINK/WONDER (VERB)

Make a 1 handshape with your dominant hand and touch the tip of your index finger to the side of your forehead while showing a thoughtful expression.

If you make a circular movement with the index finger, rather than just touching the side of the forehead, you can express a more drawn-out thinking process such as to WONDER.

THIRSTY

Make a 1 handshape with your dominant hand. Touch the tip of your index finger to the top of your throat and trace a straight line down to the bottom of your neck.

TIP: You can communicate the intensity of your thirst with an emphatic facial expression.

THRILLED (See: Excited/Thrilled/Event, page 115)

THROUGH/VIA

With both hands in flat handshapes, position the nondominant hand with the palm facing inward. Slide the dominant hand through a space between two of your nondominant fingers.

TIP: Think of something passing through your fingers.

THROUGH (TIME)

Make a 1 handshape with your dominant hand and, with the index finger pointing outward, draw a straight line to the side.

TIP: Think of how you might draw a line on a paper calendar, blocking out multiple days to indicate an event or occurrence.

THROW-UP/VOMIT

Make 5 handshapes with both hands, palms facing to the sides, and position your dominant hand close to your mouth with your nondominant hand right in front of it. Move both hands forcefully forward and downward.

TIP: Make sure your face matches what the sign is communicating.

THUNDER (See: Loud/Thunder, page 184)

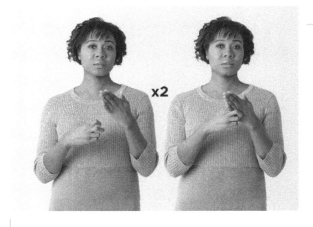

TICKET

Make a flat open handshape with your nondominant hand, palm facing inward, and make a bent V handshape with your dominant hand, palm facing to the side. Straddle the two bent fingers around the bottom of your nondominant hand, repeating the movement two times.

TIP: Imagine a ticket-taker punching a hole in a ticket.

TIGER

With both hands in 5 handshapes, touch your fingertips to your cheeks and make a gentle scratching motion, moving from your cheeks to the sides of your face.

TIP: Think of the stripes on the face of a tiger.

TIME/WHAT-TIME?

Make an S handshape with your nondominant hand and a 1 handshape with your dominant hand with a slight bend. Tap your finger on your wrist once, where your watch would be.

To turn this into WHAT-TIME?, simply put a WH? expression (page 7) on your face while signing TIME.

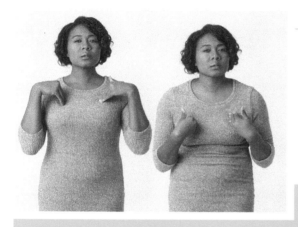

TIRED/EXHAUSTED

With both hands in flat bent hand-shapes, touch the fingertips just inside your shoulder blades and drop the hands down while maintaining contact.

TIP: People often sag their body and shoulders downward while making this sign.

TO-FILE (See: Apply/Apply-To/Application/Applicable/To-File, page 39)

TODAY (See: Now/Today, page 207)

TOILET (See: Bathroom/Restroom/Toilet, page 48)

TOMORROW

Make an open A handshape with your dominant hand and touch your cheek with the folded fingers. Arch the hand off the cheek toward the space in front of you, ending in a thumbs-up position.

TONIGHT

This sign is a combination of NOW (page 207) and NIGHT (page 204). For NOW, both hands are in Y handshapes, palms facing up. Bring the hands down quickly one time, then quickly transition into NIGHT.

For NIGHT, hold out your nondominant flat hand with the palm facing down. The dominant hand is in the bent B handshape. Place the wrist of the dominant hand on top of the nondominant hand, with the fingertips over the edge, pointing toward the floor.

TIP: When you sign NIGHT, imagine the bottom hand shows the horizon and the top hand shows the position of the sun in relation to the horizon. In this case, it's under the horizon where you can't see it.

TOOTH/TEETH/GLASS (MATERIAL)

Make an X handshape with your dominant hand and tap your index fingertip to your teeth.

TIP: To show TEETH, slide your fingertip across several teeth rather than tapping just a few.

TORNADO

Make L handshapes with both hands, thumbs extended. The palm of your non-dominant hand should face inward, and the palm of your dominant hand should face outward. Bring the tips of the thumbs together in front of your body with the hands held horizontally. Bend your index fingers two times and move the hands in a circle while signing.

TOUCH

Hold out your nondominant hand in a flat hand-shape or fist. Make a 5 handshape with your dominant hand and extend the middle finger forward to touch the back of the nondominant fist.

TOWN (See: City/Town, page 77)

TRAFFIC

Make 5 handshapes with both hands, palms facing down and your dominant hand positioned in front of your nondominant hand. Bring the hands forward in two quick stop-and-go motions.

TIP: Imagine looking down from a tall building at cars backed up in rows.

TRAIN (NOUN)

With both hands in U handshapes, palms facing down, touch the fingers of your dominant hand to the top of the fingers of your nondominant hand and rub the dominant fingers back and forth.

TRAIN (VERB) (See: Practice/Rehearse/Train, page 223)

TRANSFER

Make a bent V handshape with your dominant hand, palm facing down. Swing your wrist downward and to the side.

TIP: Imagine moving someone from one place to another.

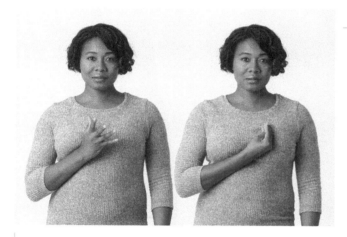

TRANSGENDER

Make a flat O handshape with your dominant hand and rest it on your heart, palm facing inward. Pull the palm away from your heart as you open your fingers, then quickly pinch them into a flat O again and rest the back of your fingers on your heart.

TRAPPED (See: Stuck/Trapped/Clogged, page 265)

TRAVEL

Make a bent V handshape with your dominant hand, palm facing down, and move the hand in a large forward-arching sweep.

TREE/FOREST

Hold out your nondominant arm in a flat handshape, palm facing down. Position your dominant elbow on the back of your nondominant hand, with the arm standing upright. Twist a 5 handshape two times with your dominant hand.

Sweep the sign to the side while repeating the movement to sign FOREST.

TIP: This sign actually looks like a tree growing from the ground, with the arm representing the trunk and the 5 handshape representing the branches of a tree.

TRUE (See: Really/True/Sure, page 229)

TRUE-BIZ (See: Fact/Sure-Enough/Real-Deal/True-Biz, page 119)

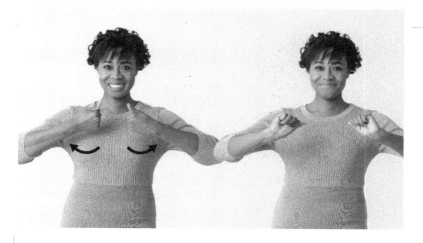

TRY/ATTEMPT

Hold out both hands in S or A handshapes, palms facing inward. Move the fists forward in a downward arching motion, ending with the palms facing outward.

TURTLE

Make an A handshape with your dominant hand and rest the palm of your nondominant hand on top of it. Wiggle the thumb of your dominant hand as if a turtle was poking its head out of its shell.

TWICE/ONCE

Make an open handshape with your nondominant hand, palm facing up, and a 2 handshape with your dominant hand, palm facing inward. Touch your dominant middle finger to the palm of your nondominant hand and swipe it inward and upward until the palm faces up.

ONCE is done with your dominant hand in a 1 handshape rather than the 2 handshape.

TWO-OF-US/US-TWO

Make a 2 handshape with your dominant hand held in front of the body, palm facing up. Move the hand back and forth, with your index finger pointing at the person you are referring to and your middle finger pointed toward yourself.

TYPICALLY (See: Tends-To/Typically, page 276)

UNCLE

Hold your dominant hand in a U hand-shape near the side of your forehead, palm facing outward but not touching your face. Make small circular or shaking motions with the hand.

UNDERSTAND/ DON'T-UNDERSTAND

Make a fist with your dominant hand and touch the thumb knuckle to the side of your forehead. Flick your index finger up two times. Think of a lightbulb turning on in your head from a good idea.

To make this DON'T-UNDERSTAND, simply shake your head in negation while signing UNDERSTAND.

UNITED-STATES (See: America/United-States, page 35)

UNIVERSE/WORLD

With both hands in U handshapes, rotate the hands around each other one time and then rest one on top of the other.

Use a W handshape for WORLD.

UNUSUAL (See: Strange/Odd/Unusual, page 263)

UP-UNTIL-NOW/ SINCE

With both hands in 1 handshapes, point your index fingertips at the shoulder of your dominant side. Move your hands forward in a downward arch, ending with your palms facing up.

UPLOAD (See: Download/Upload/Install, page 106)

UPSET

Hold your dominant hand in a flat handshape with the palm resting on your stomach. Pull your hand away from your stomach and flip it palm-up, then bring it back in so the side of the hand is now touching the stomach.

US/WE

Make a 1 handshape with your dominant hand, palm facing inward. Touch the index finger to your dominant shoulder, then arch your finger across to land on your nondominant shoulder.

US-TWO (See: Two-Of-Us/Us-Two, page 290)

USE/WEAR

Hold out your nondominant hand in a flat hand-shape, palm facing to the side or down. Make a U handshape with your dominant hand, palm facing either outward or inward, and brush the wrist in a circular motion against the back of the nondominant hand two or more times.

TIP: You do not have to change to a W handshape for WEAR; it is signed the same way as USE.

V

VALENTINE'S-DAY

With both hands in 5 handshapes, middle fingers extended forward, touch the tips of your middle fingers to your heart area and draw a heart with both hands. Follow with the sign for DAY (page 94): Hold your nondominant arm in front of your body, palm facing down. Make a 1 handshape with your dominant hand and rest the elbow on top of the fingers of your nondominant hand with your index finger pointing straight up. Drop your dominant arm down to the side to land on top of your nondominant arm.

VALUABLE (See: Important/Valuable, page 167)

VEGETABLE/VEGETARIAN

Make a V handshape with your dominant hand, palm facing outward. Touch the side of the index finger to the side of your mouth and twist the hand forward a couple of times while maintaining contact.

Add the PERSON sign (page 217) to VEGETABLE to communicate VEGETARIAN. Sign PERSON with both hands in flat open handshapes, palms facing each other but several inches apart. Bring your hands straight down several inches while maintaining the handshapes and palm orientation.

VETERANS-DAY

Fingerspell the letters V-E-T with your dominant hand, and then follow with the sign for DAY (page 94): Hold your nondominant arm in front of your body, palm facing down. Make a 1 handshape with your dominant hand and rest the elbow on top of the fingers of your nondominant hand with your index finger pointing straight up. Drop your dominant arm down to the side to land on top of your nondominant arm.

VIA (See: Through/Via, page 280)

VIDEO (See: Movie/Video, page 199)

VIEWPOINT (See: Perspective/Viewpoint, page 218)

VISIT

With both hands in V handshapes held in front of the body, palms facing inward, alternately circle your hands while keeping the palms facing inward.

TIP: You can also make this sign by moving in one forward motion.

VISUALIZE/VISION/ENVISION/IMAGINE

Make fists with both hands above your head, one in front of the other. Spread the fists apart while opening the hands into 5 handshapes until it appears like you are holding a balloon above your head.

TIP: Think of the text bubbles above characters' heads in comic books that express what the character is thinking or saying.

VOMIT (See: Throw-Up/Vomit, page 281)

WAIT

With both hands in 5 handshapes in front of the body, palms facing inward, wiggle the fingers.

TIP: If you do this sign while moving the hands simultaneously in a forward, circular movement, you indicate waiting for a long period of time.

WAKE-UP (See: Surprise/Wake-Up, page 269)

WALK

With both hands in flat open handshapes in front of your body, palms facing down, alternate moving your hands forward, as if you were taking steps.

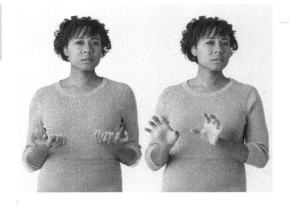

WANT/DON'T-WANT

With both hands in bent 5 hand-shapes, palms facing up, pull them toward your body while stiffening your fingers into claw handshapes.

To sign DON'T-WANT, turn the palms to face outward while shaking your head in negation.

WARM

Make a flat O handshape with your dominant hand, palm facing inward. Touch the finger-tips to your chin and move the hand upward and outward while opening the fingers into a 5 handshape.

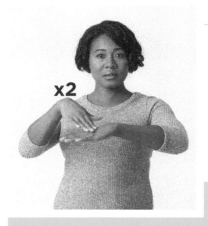

x2

WARN

Hold out your nondominant hand in a flat open handshape, palm facing down. Make a flat hand-shape with your dominant hand and tap the fingers to the back of your nondominant hand two or more times.

TIP: You can communicate the seriousness of the warning through your facial expression and sign intensity.

WASH

With both hands in A handshapes, palms pressed together, rub the fists against each other in small circular movements.

TIP: Imagine you're rubbing a washrag on a dish.

WATCH (MOVIE/TV)

Make a bent L handshape with your dominant hand in front of your body, palm facing up. Bring the hand forward in a single motion, as if holding a remote control and aiming it at the receiver.

TIP: This sign for WATCH typically refers to things that you watch that are controlled by a remote control. For things that are watched live, refer to the sign for SEE (page 238).

WATCH (WRISTWATCH)

Hold out your nondominant hand in a flat open handshape, palm facing down. Make an F handshape with your dominant hand and touch the pinched thumb and index finger to the back of your nondominant wrist two times.

TIP: The F handshape forms a circle with the thumb and index fingers, which is the shape of most watch faces.

WATER

Make a W handshape with your dominant hand and tap the side of your index finger to the front of your chin/mouth area two times.

WE (See: Us/We, page 293)

WEAR (See: Use/Wear, page 294)

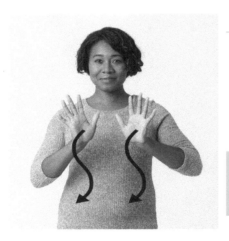

WEATHER

With both hands in 5 handshapes, palms facing outward, move the hands downward while wiggling them slightly.

TIP: Think of raindrops drizzling down a windowpane.

WEBSITE/WEB

Make a W handshape with your dominant hand, palm facing outward, and slide the hand a few inches sideways, away from the body.

TIP: Some people sign this by making three slight bounces of the hand as it moves to the side.

WEDDING

With both hands in flat open handshapes, fingers pointing down and palms facing inward, bring the hands together and end with them clasped.

TIP: Think of two hands joining together in marriage.

WEEK

Hold out your nondominant hand in a flat open handshape, palm facing up. Make a 1 handshape with your dominant hand and touch the palm to the heel of your nondominant palm. Slide the dominant hand across the palm to the fingertips.

TIP: You can incorporate how many weeks (up to 9) by incorporating a number other than 1 into this sign, such as 8 WEEKS. You can also move the dominant hand back or forward to communicate past or future, such as 3 WEEKS AGO or IN 5 WEEKS.

WEEKEND

This sign is a combination of WEEK (page 301) and END (page 113). Hold out the nondominant hand in a flat open handshape, palm facing up. Make a 1 handshape with the dominant hand and touch the palm to the heel of the nondominant palm. Slide the 1 hand across the palm to the fingertips. When you reach the fingertips, shift the 1 handshape into a flat handshape and drop it straight downward like the sign for END.

WELCOME (See: Hire/Invite/Welcome, page 158)

WEST

Hold your dominant hand up in a W handshape and move it to the left.

WHAT

With both hands in relaxed 5 handshapes, palms facing up, shake your hands side to side while furrowing your eyebrows and tilting your head slightly to the side.

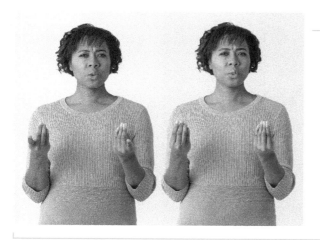

WHAT-ARE-YOU-DOING

With both hands in D handshapes, palms facing up, tap your index fingers on your thumbs two or three times. While you make this sign, furrow your eyebrows and make the "ooo" shape with your mouth, as if you were saying "do."

WHAT-FOR? (See: For/What-For?, page 132)

WHAT-KIND

Make K handshapes with both hands, one above the other. Rotate the hands around each other one time, then stop with them in a stacked position, one on top of the other.

TIP: Perform this sign with a WH? expression (page 7).

WHAT-TIME? (See: Time/What-Time?, page 283)

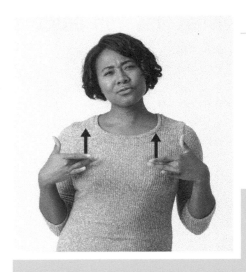

WHAT'S-UP?

With one or both hands in 5 handshapes, palms facing inward and middle fingers extended, touch both middle fingers to the sides of your chest. Move the hands upward while rotating the palms to face upward.

TIP: Your facial expression communicates the energy behind this question. Are you perhaps suspicious, curious, concerned, or just using the sign as a friendly greeting? Show it with your face.

WHEN (QUESTION)

Make 1 handshapes with both hands. Position your nondominant hand in front of the body, palm facing to the side, and position your dominant hand, palm facing down, with the tip of your finger a few inches above your nondominant hand. Circle your dominant finger around and down, ending with both fingertips touching.

WHEN (STATEMENT) (See: Happen/When [statement], page 151)

WHERE

Hold your dominant hand up in a 1 hand-shape, palm facing outward. Shake your finger side to side while furrowing your eyebrows and tilting your head.

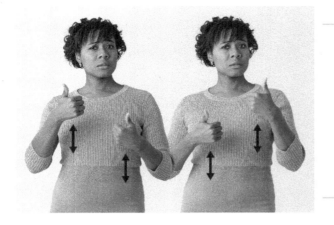

WHICH

With both hands in open A handshapes, palms facing inward, move the hands up and down in an alternating motion while furrowing the eyebrows and tilting the head.

WHILE (See: During/While, page 108)

WHO

Make an L handshape with your dominant hand, palm facing to the side, and touch the thumb to your chin. Flex the index finger open and closed a few times while maintaining a WH? expression (page 7).

WHOLE (See: All/Whole, page 31)

x2

WHY

Make a 5 handshape at the side of your forehead with your dominant hand, the middle finger extended and palm facing inward. Wiggle your middle finger up and down, furrow your eyebrows, and tilt your head to the side.

WIFE

Make relaxed C handshapes with both hands, the palm of your nondominant hand facing up and the palm of your dominant hand facing down. Touch the fingers of your dominant hand to the lower side of your face (female reference), then bring it down to clasp your nondominant hand, which is the sign for MARRIED (page 188).

TIP: HUSBAND (page 165) is signed the same way, except you touch the fingers to the upper side of the face to indicate a male reference.

WILL (VERB)

Make a flat open handshape with your dominant hand, palm facing to the side. Hold the hand next to your cheek and move it forward.

TIP: This is the sign used to indicate future tense.

WIN

Both hands start in 5 hand-shapes. Hold out your nondominant hand in a fist, palm facing to the side. With your dominant hand in a 5 handshape, palm facing to the side, brush the bottom part of the hand across the top of your nondominant fist while closing your dominant hand into a fist as well.

TIP: Think of grabbing a trophy from someone's grasp.

WIND/BREEZE

With both hands in 5 hand-shapes, palms facing each other, move your hands side to side like a breeze is blowing them.

WINE

Make a W handshape with your dominant hand. Touch the pinched fingers to your lower cheek and circle your hand two times.

WINTER

With both hands in W handshapes, palms facing outward, shake your hands side to side.

TIP: This sign is also done with fists, like the sign for COLD (page 80) but without the shivering facial expression.

WISE

Make an X handshape with your dominant hand, palm facing to the side, and wave it slightly in front of your forehead two times.

WITH

Make A handshapes with both hands, palms facing each other, and bring the fists together.

WITHOUT

Start by signing WITH: Make A handshapes with both hands, palms facing each other, and bring the fists together. Next, pull the fists apart while opening the hands into 5 handshapes.

WOLF

Make a 5 handshape in front of your nose with your dominant hand and pull the hand away from your face as the fingers close into a flat O handshape. Repeat one or two times.

TIP: Think of the long, pointed nose of a wolf.

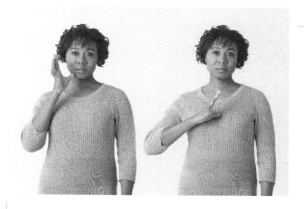

WOMAN

Make a 5 handshape with your dominant hand, palm facing to the side. Touch the thumb to your chin (female reference point), then bring the hand down and touch the thumb to the center of your chest.

TIP: MAN (page 187) is communicated by making this same sign but while touching the upper part of the face (male reference point).

WONDER (VERB) (See: Think/Wonder [verb], page 279)

WONDERFUL/GREAT

With both hands raised up in flat open handshapes, palms facing outward, tap the air in front of your hands, and then tap the air in front of your hands again a few inches lower.

WOOD

Hold out your nondominant hand in a flat hand-shape, palm facing down. Make a flat open handshape with your dominant hand and scrape it back and forth over the top of your nondominant hand two or more times.

TIP: Think of the movement of a handsaw cutting a log.

WORD

Make a 1 handshape with your nondominant hand, palm facing to the side. Make a G hand-shape with your dominant hand and touch the fingertips of the thumb and index finger to the top side of your nondominant index finger two times.

WORK

With both hands in S handshapes, palms facing down, tap the wrist of your dominant hand on the wrist of your nondominant hand two times.

TIP: Imagine hammering an iron repeatedly.

WORKOUT (See: Exercise/Workout/Gym, page 116)

WORLD (See: Universe/World, page 292)

WORRY/WORRIED

With both hands in flat B handshapes in front of your forehead, palms facing each other, move your hands in alternating circles two times.

WORSE/FIGURE-OUT

With both hands in K handshapes, palms facing each other, cross the hands, touching the fists slightly as they pass each other.

You can communicate FIGURE-OUT by making two crossing movements rather than one.

WRITE/WRITER

Hold out your nondominant hand in a flat hand-shape, palm facing up. With your dominant hand in a fist, pinch your thumb and index fingers together as if holding a pencil and draw a squiggly line across your nondominant palm.

To communicate WRITER, add the PERSON sign (page 217) to WRITE. Sign PERSON with both hands in flat open handshapes, palms facing each other but several inches apart. Bring your hands straight down several inches while maintaining the handshapes and palm orientation.

WRONG

Make a Y handshape in front of your chin with your dominant hand, palm facing inward. Start with the hand slightly away from the chin, then bring the hand toward you to touch the bent fingers to your chin as you shake your head slightly.

YEAR

Make fists with both hands, palms facing each other. Rotate the fists around each other, then stack them one on top of the other to conclude.

TIP: Think of your fists as planets rotating around each other.

x2

YES

Make a fist with your dominant hand and knock it forward two times.

TIP: You can also fingerspell the letters Y-E-S emphatically for more emphasis.

YESTERDAY

Make an A handshape with your dominant hand, palm facing outward. Touch the thumb to the side of your chin, then move the hand back and touch the thumb again near the ear.

YOU/HE/SHE/ I/ME

Make a 1 handshape with your dominant hand and point toward the person you are referring to. If you are talking about yourself, point to your chest.

TIP: When referring to people who are not present, first communicate who you are talking about, then establish a reference point for them by pointing slightly downward at a spot in the space in front of you. Continue to refer to that same spot for any ongoing pronouns related to that non-present individual. Once the topic changes, new reference points can be established for new characters of reference. In ASL, pronouns are not gender specific.

YOUNG/YOUTH

With both hands in flat bent handshapes, touch the fingertips just inside your shoulder blades and move the hands upward simultaneously two times.

YOUR/YOURS/THEIRS

Hold up your dominant hand in a flat open handshape with the fingers pointed up. Point the palm in the direction of the person you are talking about.

TIP: To sign THEIRS, sweep the hand to the side to show plural. Refer to the signing Tip for YOU (page 316) for instructions on how to refer to people who are not present. In ASL, pronouns are not gender specific.

YOU'RE-WELCOME (See: Thank-You/You're-Welcome, page 277)

YOURSELF/HIMSELF/HERSELF

Make an A handshape with your dominant hand, palm facing to the side, and push the fist forward one or two times in the direction of the person you are referring to.

TIP: Refer to the signing Tip for YOU (page 316) for instructions on how to refer to people who are not present. In ASL, pronouns are not gender specific.

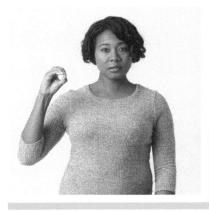

ZERO

Make an O handshape with your dominant hand, palm facing outward.

TIP: This is the same sign as the letter O, but context will usually clarify whether one is indicating the letter or the number.

ZIPPER

With both hands in pinching handshapes, touch them together toward the bottom of the chest. Move one hand straight upward while the other hand stays put.

TIP: Think of the action of zipping up a zipper while you hold the bottom in place.

ZOO

Fingerspell the letters Z-O-O with your dominant hand.

RESOURCES

To find out how to get involved with your local Deaf community, search Facebook or the web for local community groups using key words such as Deaf Community, ASL Clubs, and ASL practice or study groups, along with your city or state name. You can also check to see if there is a state organization such as (state name) Association of the Deaf. Check for community classes at local libraries and civic centers. For deeper ASL studies and language mastery, consider signing up for courses at a college or university, or get involved with their student ASL clubs/study groups.

Here is a list of additional resources for further learning:

BOOKS

Adams, Tara. *Sign Language for Kids Activity Book: 50 Fun Games and Activities to Start Signing*. Oakland, CA: Rockridge Press, 2020.

_____. *We Can Sign!: An Essential Illustrated Guide to American Sign Language for Kids*. Oakland, CA: Rockridge Press, 2020.

Fant, Louie J., Betty G. Miller, and Barbara Bernstein Fant. *The American Sign Language Phrase Book*. New York, NY: McGraw Hill, 2011.

Valli, Clayton. *The Gallaudet Dictionary of American Sign Language*. Washington, DC: Gallaudet University Press, 2005.

WEBSITES

Gallaudet University
Gallaudet.edu

National Association of the Deaf
NAD.org

Life Print University
LifePrint.com

We Can Sign
WeCanSign.com

SIGNS BY CATEGORY

Activities

Art, 41
Baseball, 47
Basketball, 47
Chat, 73
Compete/Race, 82
Dance, 93
Exercise, 116
Football, 131
Fun, 6, 138

Game, 139
Hike, 157
Magic, 186
Make, 187
Movie, 199
Music, 199
Party, 221
Play, 221
Run, 234

Shop, 67
Skill, 247
Sleep, 248
Soccer/Kick, 251
Swim, 270
Travel, 288
Walk, 10, 297
Watch (movie/TV), 299

Animals

Animal, 10, 11, 36
Bear, 49
Bird, 55
Bug, 10, 66
Butterfly, 67
Cat, 70
Cow, 89, 192

Deer, 95
Dog, 102
Elephant, 111
Fish, 129
Frog, 136
Horse, 160
Lion, 181

Monkey, 195
Pet, 218
Sheep, 241
Snake, 249
Tiger, 282
Turtle, 289
Wolf, 310

Around the House

Address, 27
Alarm, 31
Bake, 46
Bath, 48
Bathroom, 48
Bed, 51
Blanket, 56
Bowl, 59
Brush-Teeth, 65
Chair, 72
Clean, 77

Cook, 85
Couch, 87
Cup, 91
Dirty, 99
Dish, 101
Door, 105
Fork, 133
Home, 158
House, 162
Internet, 169
Kitchen, 173

Light, 180
Picture/Photo, 219
Pillow, 220
Rent, 12, 195, 231
Responsible, 232
Room, 234
Shower, 244
Spill-Cup, 256
Spoon, 257
Table, 271

Bodies

Clothes

Emotions

Events/Holidays

Food and Drink

Greetings

Medical

Money

Office/Work

People/Identifications

Places

School

Time

Travel/Vehicles

Weather/Nature

CPSIA information can be obtained
at www.ICGtesting.com
Printed in the USA
JSHW010835280422
25246JS00001B/1